THE
RAINBOW BRIDGE

First and Second Phases
Link with the Soul
Purification

By
TWO DISCIPLES

THE TRIUNE FOUNDATION

RAINBOW BRIDGE PRODUCTIONS
P.O. Box 929
Danville, CA 94526

THE SUN . . . BLACK . . . ANTAHKARANA

This formula in Teachings on Initiation in
<u>Discipleship in the New Age, Volume II</u>,
is the basis of our cover design.
The keynote as we see it is:

LET THE EARTH BECOME

A SACRED PLANET.

"The mysteries are revealed, not primarily by the reception of information anent them and their processes, but by the action of certain processes, carried out within the etheric body of the disciple. These enable him to know that which is hidden . . ."

—The Rays and the Initiations, page 337

Signed "With Love, Baba", by Sathya Sai Baba, Prashanti Nilayam, India, 1982.

INTRODUCTION TO SECOND EDITION

Changes in every part of world activity have accelerated greatly since the first printing of The Rainbow Bridge, Phase II. On the positive side, the Christ, many Masters and even Great Ones from Shamballa have taken vehicles and descended to the physical plane. This has the effect of bringing the most intense field of divine and spiritual energy to the physical plane. Since the energies of the Soul impel toward group consciousness, there is a great and growing flood of groups in all departments of human activity. It is especially notable among the New Group of World Servers, who are the intermediate groups between Hierarchy and humanity. As the effect of increased energy concentration is to produce stimulation when directed downward and transmutation when directed upward, the response of humanity has been according to their development. Both good and evil responses and activities can be seen in outer expression. This is a necessary effect and the evil which must be eliminated by the processes called Armageddon is brought to the surface, thus clearing the way for beginnings of the New Age and the Return of the Christ as a Man among Men.

Disciples are told not to fear—that Hierarchy has everything under control and that they must stand steady, hold to their linkage with the Soul and note the temporary confusion only as Observers. Thus, disciples are encouraged to think along positive lines and to contribute to the incoming New Age by creating correct and constructive thoughtforms.

TABLE OF CONTENTS

INDEX OF DIAGRAMS

COLOR PLATES

PREFACE

The Rainbow Bridge has many definitions and interpretations, both objective and subjective. It will seem to many only a poetic line dealing with ideas and images of great familiarity. On any path or road a bridge spans something which interrupts its use and the bridge becomes a part of the way.

The Path is an esoteric term used to signify the evolutionary approach to God. Since our environment, both objective and subjective, is composed of matter plus energy in a spectrum from densest matter to the freest energy, the Path is defined also as a movement in consciousness upward or inward, that is, from involvement in dense forms to those of greater freedom and beauty.

This book, the Second Phase of the <u>Rainbow</u>

Bridge series, includes the techniques of the First Phase already published in 1975. The Second Phase techniques have been given out under the supervision of several of our students who have completed the clearing processes, who are able to channel the required energies, and who are competent to teach what is necessary. Many who have followed the suggestions given in the Rainbow Bridge, Phase I, have written to the address given and received and profited by the advanced work promised. Also, there are several groups headed by our students who supervised the Second Phase work very competently. The work is thus well grounded and the thoughtforms accurate, which makes it possible to write the Second Phase which will reach the general public. This practice was followed by Dwal Khul by giving His book as lesson papers to the Arcane School before publication.

In the Rainbow Bridge, Phase I, we restated what is given in the Introductory Postulates in A Treatise on Cosmic Fire, and Proem in the Secret Doctrine, Volume I, as "acceptances" leading to "convictions." Extensions of those acceptances and convictions are covered under the heading of "Consciousness" in this book.

We received much new material as we became closer to the Ashram and able to record certain Convocations each year dealing with annual developments. Part of this we have added at the end of the book under the title "New Releases."

While this is intended as an introductory book,

there are new ideas which will be fathomed only by the advanced student. This should not discourage the novice, nor should the advanced student assume that all that is given here is already known. If discouraged, proceed to the chapters dealing with techniques, as the preceding chapters need not be understood fully at this time in the brain consciousness of the disciple for the techniques to be effective.

INTRODUCTION

We, the "Two Disciples" who wrote the Rainbow Bridge series, have had lifetimes of experience with the teachings of the Tibetan Master, Dwal Khul, who dictated many books on occult philosophy to Alice A. Bailey from 1919 to 1949. We had intimate association with Alice and Foster Bailey and their work as they implemented the teachings of the Master Dwal Khul by the printing and distribution of His many books, countless pamphlets and the invaluable work of the Arcane School. Our association with the Baileys covered all phases from the early days of the Arcane School until a few years after the death of Alice A. Bailey. Dwal Khul's efforts were to present the Ancient Wisdom, the Mystery Teachings, to the disciple-student in a suitable form adapted to modern mental development.

We belong to the New Group of World Servers, along with an increasing number of incarnating egos who are coming in to serve in the dawning New Age. We are Telepathic Communicators, as described by Dwal Khul on page 606 of A Treatise on White Magic, who prefer to work behind the scenes and acknowledge our position only when it serves the purposes of the Planetary Hierarchy during this time of transition. We both have extended perceptions of differing types and degrees and are a working team.

Our approach is based on a modern adaptation of Dwal Khul's teachings, as given through His amenuensis, Alice A. Bailey. These books have been and are our textbooks. Our work is intended to be practical above all else.

It is our intention to present the results of a lifetime of study and experiments to accomplish certain needed changes in the vehicles of the aspirant-disciple, which are required before the disciple can transmit or *ground* the energies of Externalization which are preliminary to the Return of the Christ.

It would not be out of order for us to call our work *practical experiments in the application of the Sciences of Purification, Redemption and Applied Energy, with the assistance of clairvoyant vision.* We found in the end that what we did was no contradiction of any of the techniques given by Dwal Khul, but really followed His injunction to *modify, qualify* and *adapt* the teaching.*

The techniques suggested have been thoroughly tested, first on ourselves with much learning "the hard way," and then on many cooperating students. Our testing of techniques consisted of clairvoyant observation on all personality levels, noting the effects of the meditation work done. These effects may be divided as follows:

1. Construction of the Central Channel, or Antahkarana;

2. Purification of the vehicles (bodies);

3. Redemption of energies locked into accumulated thoughtforms, desirable and undesirable;

4. Building of the Causal Body, the Soul Body, which requires material from below;

5. Certain changes in the energy flow and its mechanisms.

Dwal Khul has said that the mysteries are revealed and initiate powers gained by *changes in the vehicles* and not by the accumulation of information "anent" the mysteries; and that the liberation of the Soul comes about when the matter of the vehicles is *salvaged,* and not by the attaining of spiritual status, as usually understood.[1] Our experiments are designed to make

---

*"Disciples in all Ashrams have the task of 'modifying, qualifying and adapting the Divine Plan' simultaneously." —Discipleship in the New Age, Volume II, Alice A. Bailey, p. 389.

[1] The Rays and the Initiations, page 337; A Treatise on the Seven Rays, Volume II, page 51, by Alice A. Bailey.

those *changes in the vehicles* Dwal Khul refers to; therefore, our emphasis is on how to do it. The nature of these required changes, which must be made before the Third Initiation, and the *graded, guarded,* and *guided* processes used, are fully described in this book in such a way that even disciples who must work alone can profit thereby.

The present world crisis, resulting from the changeover from the Piscean to the Aquarian Age, presents a tremendous opportunity for progress. Since the downward, outward pressure of these externalizing energies takes advantage of every opportunity for expression, every true attempt to cooperate with the Plan of Hierarchy and the Soul meets with quick response. You may be sure that whatever capacity you have will be amplified as far as you can stand it. V'e have been told that from the standpoint of Hierarchy and the externalizing Ashram of Dwal Khul, the most important goal is to have as many disciples as possible build the Central Channel, which is the beginning of the Antahkarana. Remember, this work is aimed at increasing your capacity so that you may become more effective workers for Humanity and Hierarchy.

THE RAINBOW BRIDGE

CHAPTER I

FUNDAMENTALS

Introduction to Fundamentals

This introduction is directed to those who have little or no background knowledge of esoteric philosophy in *this* life experience. Whoever has an inkling of Soul knowledge, experience, and intuition will recognize the truth when they come into contact with it. Yet, in their legitimate effort to discriminate Truth, many disciples become dazed and confused.

Many have been misled by one or more of the cults, psychologists, mentalists, pseudo-occultists, spiritualistic communicators and mediums. Many have been instructed in teachings which have little or no foundation or which are positively misleading. These disciples often have difficulties in building a foundation of esoteric truth, and, in some cases, there is damage to their vehicles.

It must be recognized that the available, fundamental truth in the Secret Doctrine, Dwal Khul's teachings, and the various commentaries and modifications by disciples, could be the basis of a four-year college course and, if you add meditative techniques and White Magic, several years more.

Consequently, we must warn that we can only present a few concepts, some speculation, and generally accepted occult facts, without much explanation or philosophical argument, preferring to direct thought to action, to techniques, to the way to produce the changes which are the immediate goal, and which are necessary before the initiatory processes can be safely endured.

The Ancient Wisdom

The term "Ancient Wisdom" has become familiar to scholars of this century, even though they may have no specific interest in esoteric subjects. The term is vaguely associated with topics of philosophy, alchemy, secret societies, and mystery. In fact, "Mystery Teaching" is another popular name for the Ancient Wisdom. There is a persistent idea associated with the name that such mystery teaching is in the custody and understanding of enlightened human beings, sometimes referred to as Masters of the Wisdom. There are, among humanity, individuals who have an instant response to those unusual ideas and often have a sense of familiarity — almost a memory of some strange past experience.

The Ancient Teachings have always existed in symbolic form on spiritual levels.† They were placed there to assist in the evolution of the kingdoms of the Earth. In the course of the ages, periods of time in which our known history is as a day, the symbols have been brought down and their meanings "modified, qualified and adapted" to the minds and languages of those members of the human race who could profit by them. Not always have such adaptations been expressed in writing, because the ones ready for such teachings have been few, and languages (developed in terms of existing senses) were never quite adequate to clearly state the unknown— that world which we call subjective. Often, as with the sciences of today, new words had to be invented and sometimes simplified symbols were used. Communication requires not only a knowledgeable sender but an accepting, responding and qualified receiver. It is with such qualified receivers that the Brothers are concerned and never in the history of the planet have there been so many who require such guidance.

This Ancient Wisdom is not a few tattered fragments of ancient manuscript, nor is it in

†All esoteric teachers very quickly learn that teachings in words are limited to the plane of the concrete mind and that it is very difficult to translate the abstract ideas of the higher mind and the symbols of the Buddhic Plane into understandable word forms.

words, printed or spoken, nor formulated as thoughtforms of the concrete mind. It consists of energies—spiritualized forms—but something of a nature which we can barely glimpse. It is The Wisdom, and it is ancient beyond the acceptances of modern science. According to Helena Blavatsky in The Secret Doctrine (1875), there are vast libraries and commentaries on the Ancient Wisdom in existence, very much hidden and restricted. Although it is doubtful whether these libraries will ever be generally available, they can be reached by initiates whose development makes such records of value to their subsequent service. It is reported, for example, that the advent of the Planetary Hierarchy to Earth occurred 21 million years ago, followed, three million years later, by the individualization of our remote ancestor, "animal man." Thus was a relationship intensified, certainly recent by any geological standard, between individual man and his greater collective potentiality, the Hierarchy, the very Soul of the planet.

Teaching Ancient and Modern

Humanity has never, in its long history and even in its pre-history, been left without a teacher. The thread of truth has always been available to those who seek. From time to time, age after age, there have appeared Communicators, who again bring to the attention of humanity, the path to truth and life and growth in spiritual awareness. The ancient statements are as true today as they ever were; but many expansions, adaptations, and interpretations, according to the need of any given time in man's growth, have been successfully given. It must never be forgotten that many of these statements and interpretations have been given through men, however dedicated and sincere, and because of this, these teachings have varied somewhat in the telling. Nevertheless, the truth is *there* and available to discriminating students.

We are entering a new field of knowledge, applicable to disciples in all departments of human activity and Dwal Khul's teachings are the Hierarchical adaptation of the Ancient Wisdom to suit such changed objectives and disciples. This means that older and even most contemporary teachings are not as well suited, in spite of the high quality of some in relation to earlier disciples and circumstances.

Communicators appear to direct the aspirations of men; they have done so in every past era and are doing so now. Such is the Master Dwal Khul, the Tibetan, who, as a former teacher known to us as Confucius, left the enduring imprint of His thought upon Chinese philosophy. As the great teacher, Aryasanga, He left numerous works in Tibet which have also influenced an entire people.

Today this Master of Wisdom and Compassion has again given humanity, through numerous works,* a modern presentation of the ancient truths with deeper interpretation; these works will provide the basis of a teaching which will find expression in the anticipated New Age of Aquarius which is now beginning with the world "housecleaning" seen everywhere.

Since, as has been accepted by science, *all is energy,* or matter which may be converted into energy and energy into matter, the Ancient Wisdom is presented by Dwal Khul as "The Science of Applied Energy," dealing with the mental concepts and processes through which man's evolution may be "enforced." As the "Science of Purification," He deals with the processes of the emotional nature and the hindering accumulations of mistaken or outworn creations and thoughtforms vitalized by desire in man's emotional nature. Under the heading "The Science of Redemption" He deals with the release of energy-substance from the accumulation of past creations on all personality levels. In this way, the personal self provides redeemed matter which the Soul uses as a reservoir of power or to build the "Body of Light." Our closed group has successfully demonstrated, as far as has been individually possible, the existence and application of the three sciences described briefly above and in the book called The Externalization of the Hierarchy, page 693,

*The many books Dwal Khul has presented through His amenuensis, Alice A. Bailey, available either in hardback or softback in most bookstores handling spiritual or metaphysical literature, are also available from the Lucis Publishing Company, 113 University Plaza, 11th floor, N.Y., NY 10003.

written by Dwal Khul.

We have said that all we teach is in what Dwal Khul has written and that he has said it better than we can say it. However, we are trying to fill a gap, not so much in teaching *about* the subject as in calling attention to beginning techniques, by the use of which, the student-disciple can make necessary changes in his personality elements (vehicles). According to ancient practices, intermediate incarnated teachers are needed to indicate the next step forward and to extend a helping-hand when needed by aspirants. This indicates that, in the interest of efficiency and communication, such assisting teachers must not be too far ahead of their students in the chain of Hierarchy.

It may be helpful at this point to explain the creative process by which Hierarchy inaugurates a new teaching, in this case the teaching for the New Age. There is much speculation on this matter, and many claims are made purporting to be the fountainhead of the New Age, but the keys to understanding when and how such teaching is to be given are explained in the books of the Tibetan Master.

As to the time factor, the principal contributions to the teaching are made at fifty-year intervals, that is, 1875, 1925 and 1975. Although, on the mental and higher planes, *time as we know it does not exist,* we must consider these points in time as being cyclic repetitions on the mental plane. Since, on that plane, it is not a simple cycle like a sine wave, but a composite, we cannot always interpret on the physical level if the emerging teaching will climax exactly at the dates given. In truth, the teaching of the New Age began a long time ago, as we, bound to the past, present and future concepts of the physical world, must consider.

In 1875, through H. P. Blavatsky, the Tibetan Master, acting as the "front man" for Hierarchy, as He called Himself, and more directly for the three Masters who will hold office when the New Age is in full bloom (Morya, Koot Humi and Rakoczi), gave the world the Secret Doctrine.

In 1925, as the Tibetan Master had planned, He gave, through Alice A. Bailey, the psychological key to understand the Secret Doctrine. Along with this, He also outlined certain other keys which will be "turned" at the cyclic points mentioned (the astrological key, for instance). The revelations of the psychological key were spread over thirty years. Those who study cycles recognize that energies are not released in a single explosion, but are released at a gradually increasing tempo which climaxes and then decreases. We are *now* in the increasing phase of the 1975 cycle, and we should take note of world events confirming this fact.

Times are changing, and because the rational mind has no solution to world and individual problems, students and seekers are turning to the subjective worlds—the subjective source of all that is tangible and objective.

There are those who consider that once a truth

is put into writing, it becomes sacred. Its form then becomes crystallized and permanent, any change unthinkable, any experiment anathema, and the precious form to be handled reverently only by a dedicated priestcraft, which quickly erects a structure through which all communications must pass. This should not be allowed to happen to the teachings of Dwal Khul.

There is, of course, a penalty when a new presentation of Truth is given to the unqualified, and to the publication media generally; it will be misinterpreted, plagiarized, rewritten for profit, combined with false and unsuitable teachings of the past, used in injurious directions, divided into sects, and otherwise abused. Unfortunately, there are very few teachers equipped to lead the inquirer safely through the incredible maze of current so-called occult literature and expose the number of false prophets.

Consequently, it is our goal for all students to approach occult study with an open mind, ready to accept that which is good and reject that which is false, invoking their own Soul and in the wisdom of the Soul, desire to know the truth, then confidently expect that illumination which is the result of contact with the higher mind. When this contact is made, it will not be forgotten, and the student will find *within himself the Touchstone of Truth. This is our goal for students. Let the day come when you will stand on your own feet, recognize your own duty and responsibility and ask no one to make decisions for you, here, hereafter, inner or outer. Collec-*

*tively students will help to build the world
Antahkarana as they grow individually, and this
is the larger goal and the mainspring of our
emphasis.*

We conclude, therefore, with what the Lord
Buddha has said: ". . . that we must not believe
in a thing said merely because it is said; nor tradi-
tions because they have been handed down from
antiquity; nor rumors, as such; nor writings by
sages, because sages wrote them; nor fancies that
we may suspect to have been inspired in us by a
Deva (that is, in presumed spiritual inspiration);
nor from inferences drawn from some haphazard
assumption we may have made; nor because of
what seems an analogical necessity; nor on the
mere authority of our teachers or masters. But
we are to believe when the writing, doctrine, or
saying is corroborated by our own reason and
consciousness. 'For this,' says He in concluding,
'I taught you not to believe merely because you
have heard, but when you believed of your consciousness, then to act accordingly and abun-
dantly.'"‡

---

‡Secret Doctrine, Volume III, page 401 by H. P. Blavatsky.

CHAPTER II

BEGINNINGS

It is probably not necessary to consider such abstract matters as the meanings of time, space, matter, spirit, motion, and energy, and so on, in this book. And yet, when beginners ask what the Ancient Wisdom says concerning these subjects, it seems necessary to try to answer these questions in as comprehensible a manner as possible. Textbooks on these subjects become so involved as to be most frustrating to the concrete mind. There is much available material which tries to analyze these abstract matters, from ancient records up to Einstein and his many interpreters. These voluminous writings have not been neglected by the authors, but in the end we return to Dwal Khul.

Everything begins with *space*, from whence all things proceed and into which all things disappear; in such vast cycles of time the years appear in fifteen digit figures or more.

Space is an entity says Blavatsky. This brings us face to face with the fact that there are no absolutes. *Nothing is absolutely so.* We must consider points of view of a very long series of *observers,* from ourselves to some vast ultimate entity far beyond our comprehension. For all these observers, *space is that which appears to be emptiness.* We emphasize that which *appears* to be emptiness to a particular observer. It is that which is above and beyond, and which changes as the observer changes. As the vehicles become more refined, and the quality of the atoms of which they are built become of a higher vibration, perception changes and what had appeared to be emptiness is filled with a new level of being and inhabitants thereof. Each step is "Life more Abundant" on the Jacob's Ladder of *evolution.* It is at this point that the ancient statement of the Emerald Tablet of Hermes,

> *"that which is above is as*
> *that which is below . . ."*[†]

states a law which is a necessary foundation for understanding. Space to us appears to be empty, but science acknowledges its fullness. In anything higher, there appears to be an emptiness to that which is below it. So, the ultimate "space" is not empty at all, but is filled with life, and is an "entity" to which all things go in evolu-

---

[†]A Treatise on Cosmic Fire, by Alice A. Bailey, p. 1066. Originally from the Emerald Tablet of Hermes.

tion, and from which all things proceed in involution.

God Concepts

Space could, therefore, be called God, since in its fullness it contains all power, all knowledge, and is everywhere present. We must conclude from this that, by the Law of Analogy, no limit is reached and observation disappears into infinity. Paraphrasing the Master Koot Humi, in The Mahatma Letters to A.P. Sinnet, in Letter X, speaking for Hierarchy, He says that *there is nothing but Nature and Natural Law.* Thus, He denies all human God Concepts and goes on to state that two-thirds of evil (for humanity) comes from false God concepts, promoted by clever minds to enslave humanity. There is no God, no one intelligent entity outside His creation: *There is only Nature manifesting through its immutable laws.* The only true "priest" is *the one who can demonstrate in himself something of the nature of God.* Since there is a succession of observers, a succession of expanding awareness and perception, there is also a series of those who can demonstrate the nature of God in ascending capacity, each a God to that which is below him, although never the ultimate.[1]

---

[1]Dwal Khul states the God Idea as INTRODUCTORY POSTULATE I in A Treatise on Cosmic Fire, page 3: *"There is one Boundless Immutable Principle; one Absolute Reality which antecedes all manifested conditioned being. It is beyond the range and reach of any human thought or expression.* The manifested Universe is contained within this Absolute Reality and is a conditioned symbol of it."

Involution — Multiply

According to the Mystery Teachings, in the beginning, our *ultimate* observer saw in the solidity of apparent "nothingness" an appearance of something like uniform bubbles, the shape water takes when air is blown into it. They were in random motion, and in their collisions they sometimes repelled and sometimes attracted and clumped or grouped. The distance apart seemed to have something to do with attraction, and motion with repulsion. This beginning of evolution, for that is what it is, has been called *The Great Breath,* which, when withdrawn takes all creation with it. It should be noted, that the term evolution in this use includes involution, which then relates to form building, multiplication, the outgoing breath, leaving evolution to apply to the indrawn breath or the *return to Nature,* the true God idea.

The bubble appearance was not as a film enclosing space or gas, but as if in a spherical volume something was separated from an area of space which condensed into a spot in the center. That which remained was still a space, but the condensed center was the beginning of substance or ultimately—*Matter.* That area of space deprived to produce matter belonged with it and the pair of opposites, *Spirit-Matter* was born. *Everything appears as a result of the first manifestation, Spirit-Matter, and its product—Consciousness.* These activities in space were in sequence, and thus produced the first unit of Time.

SPIRIT — MOTION — MATTER
LIFE — CONSCIOUSNESS — FORM

NATURE

YANG ——|||—— YIN

SPIRIT	MATTER
LIGHTNESS	DARKNESS
CAUSE	EFFECT
TANMATTRAS	TATTVAS
COMING	GOING

WITHOUT MOTION THEY WOULD MERGE AND CEASE
NOTHING IS ABSOLUTELY SO
ONLY GOD IS PERFECT
The Two Primary Principles Locked in Eternal Motion

DIAGRAM 1

Before this sequence there was only duration, an aspect of space, the eternal *now*.

We have ended with an enlarged symbol of the Yin and Yang, which represent opposites, interlocked and twined in motion. The units of attraction and repulsion are brought together in this symbol, but kept separate by motion. This corresponds to the Life-Consciousness-Form trinity. Spirit combines with matter to produce a third entity, Consciousness.

Thus, we have our surrounding universe built of units of attraction and repulsion and *motion,* in that undefinable matrix we call *Nature* or *God.* This has been called *Space, nothingness, the void.* It is said that the element of space called spirit has the quality of space at any level and, therefore, identification with it can lead consciousness back to the source.

Anyone interested in the philosophical aspects of the problem should start with the Secret Doctrine which relates it to the original records as far as possible. Our comments are far from the complexities involved in the text of the Secret Doctrine or other speculations, but it should convey the idea of a vast appearance of nothingness in which an orderly process or sequence of events developed within itself units of attraction and repulsion, combining then into what our senses now perceive within that same original space.

The countless steps between *Space* and the visible *Universe* within it are described in the volumes and libraries of the Ancient Wisdom.

Evolution — Unify

This is a reverse process in which the multiple manifestations wherein we live, move, and have our being, return to the original appearance of nothingness—*Space.*

The situation is further complicated by the fact that both *involution* and *evolution* are going on at the same time within *our* observation, within ourselves and in our environment. It means, apparently, that it is useless for us to try to understand it *as we are,* but since we are part of it, our understanding will grow *as we grow,* or *evolve.*

In this impasse we are comforted by the statements in the Ancient Wisdom that we lose nothing, retaining what we will, but gaining by the expanding union in steps which lead to the ultimate union in Space itself. Perhaps if we call it *God* our mystical aspirations will be satisfied.

Our problem is that we try to think in absolutes which do not exist. *All is relative*—even illusion.

Consider, for example, the Yin-Yang symbol, in which we find the elements of the Mutable Cross. It is easier to express the imperfections in the Yin-Yang symbol by the infusion of the opposite quality in the form of small circles or dots. The quality or consciousness element in the Yin-Yang is its *motion,* without which the opposites would merge; the form would disappear into *Nature,* which alone has the quality called *Omnipresence,* appearing or disappearing according to its immutable laws in all its manifestations.

CONDITION OF UNBALANCE

YANG   **YIN**

THE PAPER
REPRESENTS NATURE

All processes are aimed at perfect accomplishment and all systems which we recognize are moving in time and space towards some goal with rhythmic activity implying perfection to be attained but not yet actual and the intelligent consciousness thereof (God) is not yet perfect in expression.

All in nature will be, is, or has been human. Therefore, all gods have been human, and you are all you know of God *now*.

DIAGRAM 2

Although all is illusion, we must accept our illusions as temporary facts. We see the objects around us as solid and substantial, avoiding the now known *fact* that they are nothing of the kind. If we were suddenly reduced in size to molecular dimensions we would find ourselves in

a world of energy systems. They were there all
the time and the appearance of density or solidity
was *relative* because of the limitations of our
serses. We could sum it up by saying *illusion is a
most important limitation for our sanity.*

In spite of the illusive nature of everything, we
must try to discover what there is in it which is
analogous to that which is above:

1. Everything is made of units, infinitesimally
   smaller than we have been able to measure;

2. These units combine and the combination is
   a *unit* in a larger structure;

3. This process of unification into successively
   larger and more complicated structures or
   units continues to the kingdoms, the
   planets, the systems, the galaxies, the
   Universe;

4. It is a multiple process in which all steps
   exist at the same time in our observation;

5. The human kingdom is just one of the required steps in evolution; therefore, we can
   state, along with the Ancient Wisdom, that
   *everything in the Universe is now, has been,
   or will be human.*

EVOLUTION IS THE PATH OF RETURN

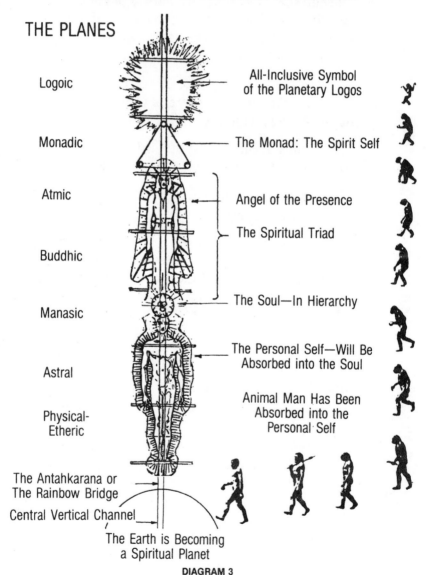

THE PLANES

Logoic — All-Inclusive Symbol of the Planetary Logos

Monadic — The Monad: The Spirit Self

Atmic — Angel of the Presence

The Spiritual Triad

Buddhic

Manasic — The Soul—In Hierarchy

The Personal Self—Will Be Absorbed into the Soul

Astral

Animal Man Has Been Absorbed into the Personal Self

Physical-Etheric

The Antahkarana or The Rainbow Bridge

Central Vertical Channel

The Earth is Becoming a Spiritual Planet

DIAGRAM 3

CHAPTER III

CONSCIOUSNESS

The Acceptances and Convictions*

Among the students who follow the techniques offered in this book with success, certain acceptances and convictions are frequently evidenced as part of the student's consciousness:

1. There is *One* all-inclusive, powerful Principle, Life, Being, Existence, Intelligence, God.

2. There is a Law of Rebirth or Cyclic Return. Reincarnation is a fact.

3. There is a Law of Cause and Effect or Karma.

---

*In the Preface of this book we commented on the relation between Dwal Khul's Introductory Postulates in A Treatise on Cosmic Fire, page 74, and have decided to include from Rainbow Bridge, Phase I "The Acceptances," with a few changes, even if there is some duplication of material.

4. There is a Law of Unification on the Path of Return. All Souls are unified in the One Soul of Humanity.

These Acceptances underlie all of our work but do not, as yet, have clear recognition in the brain consciousness of most students. Response to our simplified version of the "secret doctrine" will vary. The more purification and clarity existing in individual students the more quickly will response in the form of understanding come. We expect all students to look to the *sources* of the information we give with eagerness and response. What we warn against is the smug response that "we know this already." There will be familiar teaching or so it will appear, but what we have to say is linked to *process* which is distinctly *not familiar* as the condition of the vehicles, the life environment and the aura invariable show. From the very beginning, the emphasis of our work has been placed upon processes and *how* to grow spiritually, even to the neglect, somewhat, of the fundamentals "about" occult teaching. For the present, we shall confine ourselves to what The Light of the Soul calls, on page 123, "spiritual reading."

ACCEPTANCE NUMBER ONE
There is One All-Inclusive, All Powerful
Principle, Life, Being, Existence, Mind, God.

It is generally accepted by intelligent people everywhere that there is a guiding principle operative in the Universe, no matter by what name it is called or recognized. Order and system and plan in the unfoldment of nature—mineral, vegetable and animal, as well as human—is known and accepted by scientists, religionists and others today, at least under the term "natural law." The Universe is growing, expanding and developing, and this is well known. This used to be a mere belief, an emotional response, but this is no longer the case. Knowing relates to the development of mind, which has become widespread in this century.

All scientific thought has always sought a simple beginning, a basic unit from which all things are made. This thought has progressed far, but not yet as far as the ancient teaching, which says in effect that *Space* was the beginning, and that units of attraction and repulsion appeared therein and proceeded by their simple qualities, plus motion, to build all forms and time and space itself as we seem to know them. This is the startling addition: all forms, both objective and subjective—spirit, mind and emotion and all qualities good and bad—are also products of this awesome simplicity.

Is it not to be expected that this will be accepted with something like shock? (The Tibetan Master says the truth *can be* terrifying.) If it is recognized that goodness, and beauty, and truth come from this oneness of beginning, why should the processes of involution and evolution be terrifying and unacceptable? Is the anthropomorphic God less horrifying with His balancing counterpart in the form of the Devil, in their unexplained and irrational relationship to the poor clay which they have modelled, and with which they play their ghastly games of life and death with Hell and Heaven behind the goal posts? The disciple does not choose with superstition.

In mankind, blinded by the fogs of superstition and belief, there is a common aspiration to something better and higher if only in terms of material living, emotional satisfaction, and mental awakening. Such aspiration is lighted by the conviction and intuition that beneath all manifestation there is plan and purpose, and though they may not discern the ultimate Being, they are sure that there is love and joy to be found and won on the journey of life to which they are unknowingly committed, and that there is a Kingdom, and a Power, and a Glory awaiting their conscious awareness and experiencing.

ACCEPTANCE NUMBER TWO
There is a Law of Rebirth or Cyclic Return.
Reincarnation is a fact.

The Law of Rebirth is a concept quite generally accepted by thoughtful people everywhere today. One reason for general acceptance is human recognition of the fact that no one is perfect at the end of any one life, and that many opportunities are needed to unfold the perfect, inclusive consciousness planned for mankind.

None of us has ever known a human being, however good, who had no weaknesses and no need to deepen his consciousness. And so we have, in the plan, infinite opportunity for experience and the growth into perfect consciousness.

This acceptance is known by the disciple as an innate conviction; the form is not the Life, and there is an essence which continues, which is not the trivialities of memory which seem to form the personal self. These memories recorded in the computer cells of the physical brain, have no future beyond those cells, except as some essence which may be extracted by more subtle forms when the outworn shell with its gossamer web of cells is left behind.

Who remembers, or cares to remember, the infinite detail of yesterday's action? If there is that which binds desire, desire will build anew in another place with another name. The Law is just and accurate, and there is endless time patiently to repeat that which is needed; many shells are left on the shores of Life's boundless sea.

Reincarnation is a fact, yes, but what incarnates again, the mouldering dust of forgotten graves, the swirls of spent emotion, the shapes of half-formed thought? Not these, the lost, but that which used them, the Shining One (the Soul) enduring in its irridescent palaces, striving downward to awaken in the mind of Earth that which will stir and build itself a garment suitable for Gods.

ACCEPTANCE NUMBER THREE

There is a Law of Cause and Effect. *

ACCEPTANCE NUMBER FOUR

There is a Law of Unification on the Path of Return. All Souls are Unified in the One Soul of Humanity.

Many sense the fact that all Souls are part of the one human Soul, but this fact is not yet generally recognized and accepted. This causes certain segments of the human race to feel superior to certain others and to hold unreasonable prejudices. There has been a great deal of talk and thought about brotherhood, but very little practice of the concept as yet. Ultimately, when etheric vision is more generally developed in humanity, individuals will know their fundamental brotherhood as Souls and act from knowledge, rather than from belief.

That all Souls are unified is not a "becoming," it is the *present truth*. All are brothers on the level of Soul. The Path of Return is a path of conscious awakening to a divine fact. Here, we are separate, parted by the shells of form which are pierced by arrows of feeble senses for crippled communication. We can see, "as through a glass darkly," a distorted vision. Yet, these same senses, developed slowly and consecu-

---

*This Acceptance is discussed at length under the heading "The Law of Cause and Effect."

tively by the painful impacts of a brutal evolution of form, are a promise of the future. The veils grow thin; the higher correspondences are there to be won, they *must* be won. There are many among the young, the "Children of the Dawning Age," who glimpse with wonder the light behind the form, the swirling glory that waits recognition, the glowing signs of that which waits, the rim of Heaven's World.

These four Acceptances are inherent in disciples. Sometimes, however, they are not as clearly recognized by students who express their ideas in less philosophical and a more direct form—in their convictions. Not all persons, no matter how *nice,* nor how many years of reading and studying are in their background can do the purifying work successfully. Only those, including the young and unlearned, can do this work who have certain built-in convictions which are the outer evidence of an inner state of consciousness and development. These convictions are usually expressed by the student who is ready to begin this work and, as given here, provide some guidance to those who are forming groups:

The Convictions are:

1. A belief in the continuity of life and consciousness.

2. A conviction that there is something in or above which is higher or deeper and worth striving for.

3. A certainty that there is a way to reach this

higher consciousness.

4. An acceptance that there is a way involving methods of thought, feeling and action which can change the future and improve the conscious self.

5. An intuitive vision of the fact that there must be those who have found the way and succeeded. Some persons will recognize the different scale and variation of knowledge of those around them, some knowing a great deal more and some knowing a great deal less than themselves. Some persons will recognize that some have found the way and mastered all to be known through the evolution of man, the Masters. Others will think of them as members of the White Brotherhood, or of the Planetary Hierarchy.

6. A sense of personal responsibility to make the effort in spite of all personal obstacles. This means a willingness to devote time, money, energy, and a one-pointed attention or whatever seems likely to speed progress to the goal.

7. A motivation, not only for self-improvement but for service—to be able to serve others with what is gained.

8. There is generally a demonstration by students of these convictions in their attitudes and responses in the events of their lives.

Consciousness

All units are *conscious.* We define conscious-ness in that which is below us in evolution as being the apparently fixed reactions to environ-ment. It is also called subconscious. For our-selves, we say self-conscious. For above, super, or Soul-consciousness. Beyond that, identifi-cation or Monadic or Logoic consciousness, and so on.

The word consciousness relates to the relation-ship between *spirit* and *matter,* or between a higher or a lower unit, the higher being nearer the spirit and thus partaking of its nature, and the lower unit being relatively nearer the nature of matter.

The basic trinity which Dwal Khul refers to is *Life-Quality-Appearance.* We use *Life-Con-sciousness-Form* because of the relative famil-iarity of those words. They are synonymous, but require some explanation to show the broad application from the mineral kingdom to God. Life as space is everywhere. Form is relative to environing conditions, for example, ice, water, steam. Consciousness is the relation of life to form, expressed in movement and behavior. We define the consciousness of the mineral kingdom as its *habitual behavior.* To say that this is ex-plained by the discerned laws of chemical or physical reaction merely calls attention to the fact that these actions are according to the *Laws of Nature* and that the laws also apply to all higher forms of consciousness, even those which

Dwal Khul calls *Identification,* apologizing for the difficulty in finding an understandable definition.

We use the word consciousness in the sense that Blavatsky used it—*time is a succession of states of consciousness.* Thus, when we turn to our Cosmic Physical Plane:

THE MINERAL KINGDOM

The consciousness of the mineral kingdom is expressed by its normally slow sequence of events, for its consciousness is only its habitual reaction to its environment, whether to the units of the mineral kingdom or to applied energy. Duration for the mineral kingdom exists, to a limited extent, but only for its group Soul.

THE VEGETABLE KINGDOM

Consciousness demonstrates in increased sensitivity to environment and a great multiplicity of forms. It is said that the vegetable kingdom, within itself, has reached a much higher state of evolution than some of the other kingdoms.

Any evidence of duration lies in what is called the Group Soul of these two kingdoms. The evidence of planning is very definite in the crystalline forms of the mineral kingdom and in the burgeoning multiplicity of forms in the vegetable kingdom.

THE ANIMAL KINGDOM

The animal kingdom is said to function almost entirely through instinct, which can be described as automatic reaction and which does show some evidence of anticipation of the future besides that of its Group Soul.

THE HUMAN KINGDOM

In the human kingdom, consciousness is defined as "self-consciousness," and the capacity to create thoughtforms, combining memory, anticipation and desire. This is a more definite manifestation of duration.*

Beyond this we have Soul consciousness, then, on the Monadic level, Identification, and finally, the All-Inclusive consciousness of the Logos.

THE PLANES AND THE RAYS

It has already been mentioned that space is a fullness in an area which appears to be empty. It is implicit that whatever comes from space, is in there already, in some archetype, perhaps as some ultimate unit of an undefinable nature. Beginning with a cycle of activity, a series of events starting with a differentiation of space into Spirit and Matter, with their interaction which is called consciousness, the visible Universe was produced by this process called *involution*. There is at this

---

*The nature of duration and its relation to time is considered more fully under the title "The Law of Cause and Effect."

time, a reversal of this process and a gradual reabsorbing of the spirit-matter manifestation until nothing is left but the original space from which it came. This is *evolution,* or a return to God, or *Space,* which has the characteristics usually ascribed to Deity.

By the time involution reached the ultimate and turning point, a minor and, according to size, relatively unimportant solar system developed characteristics which form the basis of all our knowledge. It is said that this knowledge is available to the Masters, and that They know all that can be known of this solar system. It is from this repository that available teachings come.

We have reproduced a portion of a diagram from A Treatise on Cosmic Fire, page 94, by Dwal Khul, which indicates the involutionary-evolutionary cycle and the dip into dense matter. This refers to the righthand part of the diagram. This great cycle, covering literally countless years of time, is inclusive of the entire manifested Universe, and countless Universes which are not visible to our senses. The great cycle is also sevenfold in character, and the nature and quality of its divisions conform to the ancient statement already given: *"that which is above is as that which is below . . . "*[†]

The lefthand side of Diagram 4 refers to the process of redeeming the dense matter of the lower planes. This is done first in the vehicles of disciples and finally in humanity as a vehicle of the Logos.

[†]A Treatise on Cosmic Fire by Alice A. Bailey, p. 1066.

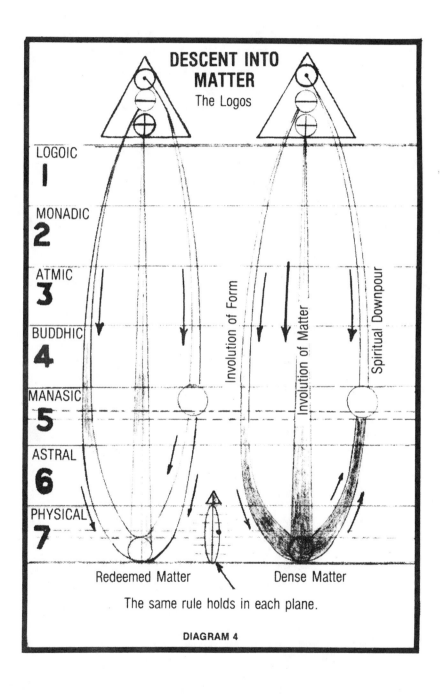

DESCENT INTO MATTER
The Logos

1 LOGOIC
2 MONADIC
3 ATMIC
4 BUDDHIC
5 MANASIC
6 ASTRAL
7 PHYSICAL

Involution of Form

Involution of Matter

Spiritual Downpour

Redeemed Matter

Dense Matter

The same rule holds in each plane.

DIAGRAM 4

Our solar system appears to ordinary sense perception to consist of a central sun with planets in orbit around it against a background of emptiness having the appearance of original space. Yet, it is not "empty" space, as it appears. Within space are spirit/matter combinations in seven gradations, from what appears to be almost pure spirit to almost pure matter. These are relative terms, for we know that the octave or background of spirit/matter energies is only one of the many octaves above and below it. The range of attenuated matter, at the upper extremity, and dense matter, at the lower extremity, which separates into seven octaves is called *The Planes*. We refer here to a diagram called The Great Spectrum, which gives the names and relationships of these planes.

Each one of these seven planes of our solar sysem is subdivided into seven subplanes, and each of these being divided into seven again. For example, the physical plane is subdivided into three areas which are most familiar, that is, the solid, liquid and gaseous. Beyond those, however, are the not generally recognized, more rarified, zones of matter plus energy, which we call the subetheric level. Beyond that is a similar area called the super-etheric, then the subatomic, and finally at the upper extremity of our physical plane is an area which we call the atomic. These are the seven subplanes of this physical plane.

We must point out here that the four upper subplanes of the physical plane constitute the energy aspect of the physical body and that the

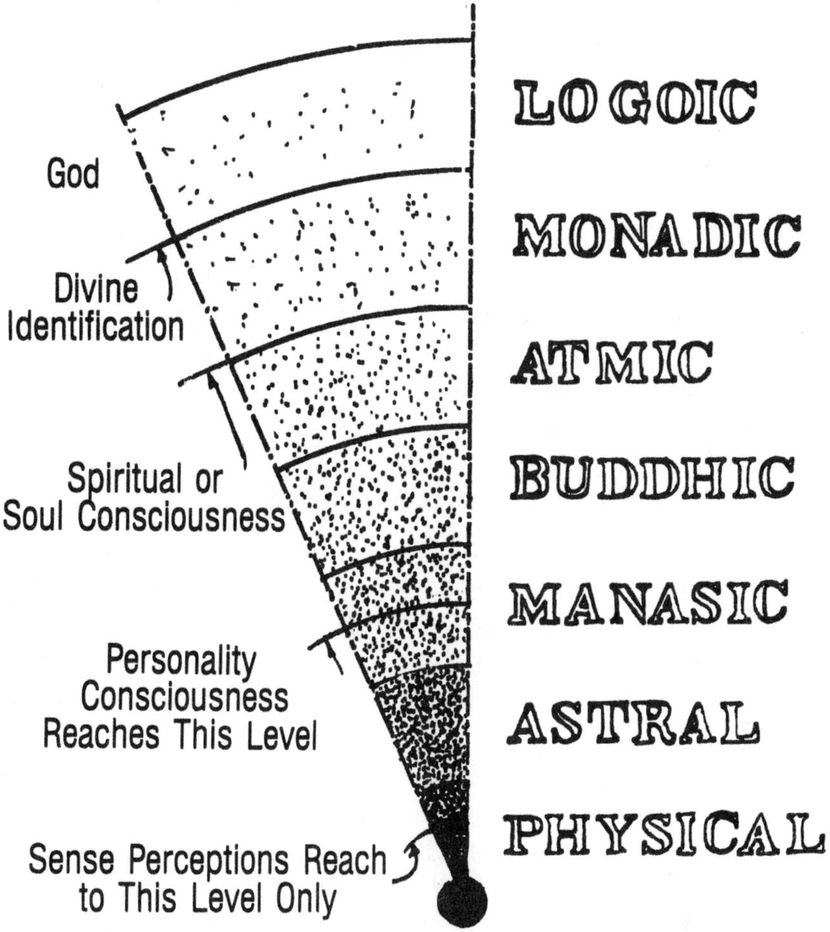

God

Divine
Identification

Spiritual or
Soul Consciousness

Personality
Consciousness
Reaches This Level

Sense Perceptions Reach
to This Level Only

LOGOIC

MONADIC

ATMIC

BUDDHIC

MANASIC

ASTRAL

PHYSICAL

THE GREAT SPECTRUM
(COSMIC PHYSICAL PLANE)

DIAGRAM 5

lower three—solid, liquid and gaseous—constitute the solid portion of the physical body. As a
whole, the energy body, or the etheric body,
dominates and controls the lower three subplanes
or solid physical body. From an esoteric standpoint, the energy body, or etheric body, is the
real physical.

The point to be made here is that the qualities
of each plane have a correspondence to the higher
sevenfold divisions. When the disciple has made
the changes in his vehicles that make understanding possible, he must understand the relation between the planes and the subplanes and
the application of the Law of Analogy in order to
become an effective White Magician.

It should be kept in mind that these diagrams
are two-dimensional tools used to portray the
concept of the various divisions of the ratio of
energy to matter. It is misleading to consider the
planes as layers with barriers or lines between.
The gravitational separation around a center,
man, or planet, gives the same suggestion; for
the heaviest matter-energy substance is nearer the
center of attraction. In truth, the higher, more
subtle matter-energy *interpenetrates* the lower at
all points, like water in a bucket of sand and the
ultimate subdivision is *space*. Even the water-in-
sand analogy is misleading for the subtle is not
impeded by the gross except where it is the
foundation of a form.

While the planes are related to the fields of the
seven stars of the Constellation Pleiades, the
Rays, on the other hand, are directed energy

emanations from the Constellation Ursa Major, or the Great Bear. These energies are directed into the solar system in a triangular pattern through the zodiacal signs, and there to the Sun, and then to the planets involved. There are seven of these Rays, which relate to the seven planes of spirit-matter, depending upon what level they appear.

It should be remembered that since all energy emanates from the One Source, all energy is spiritual. There are seven avenues of expression, or seven frequencies of energy which are tabulated as follows:

RAY 1—
WILL OR POWER
Symbol: The Sword or Baton

Government and Politics; International Relations; Executive Action.

RAY 2—
LOVE-WISDOM
Symbol: The Crossed Pens

Education & Teaching. Communication, using the media; writing, speaking, radio, television and audio-visual methods.

RAY 3—
INTELLIGENT ACTIVITY
Symbol: The Spider Web

Finance, Trade, Business, Economics in all its aspects including manipulations. All other human activities (the last four Rays on the physical level of life stem from or are related to this Ray because they are Rays of Quality and are specialized types of intelligent activity.)

RAY 4—
HARMONY THROUGH
CONFLICT
Symbol:The Balance or Scales

Sociology, including race and culture; application of the principles of cooperation and conciliation. Creative aspiration as expressed through all the arts.

RAY 5—
CONCRETE MIND
AND SCIENCE
Symbol: The Crucible

The human capacity to think, plan, design, concentrate, reconstruct the world and all else. The Sciences, including medicine and psychology.

RAY 6—
IDEALISM & DEVOTION
Symbol: The Chalice

Religion and Ideology; Philosophy. All concepts and aspirtion for the good and true.

RAY 7—
ORGANIZATION AND
RITUAL; MAGIC;
EXTERNALIZATION
Symbol: The Crystal; The
Torch, The Energy of Life

Structuring of society through Institutions and the ordering of Power through Ceremony, Protocol, and Ritual.

This tabulation of Ray qualities, while only a brief description, gives a suggestion of the qualities which are produced by the Ray-Plane relationship. It is a combination like Spirit-Matter, which produces consciousness, or in the case of the Rays—quality. Both the Planes and the Rays are ensouled by lives, the substance of each consisting of myriads of tiny lives, all being responsive to the larger Life which ensouls them.

There is a polarity relationship between the Planes and the Rays. It is symbolized by the statement that the Seven Pleiades are the seven wives of the Seven Rishis of the Great Bear. Such relationship is always productive of a third entity—the Sun or Consciousness. Accordingly, the Plane field in which our planet functions is influenced by a directed Ray energy to make a new energy field. The Ray energies enter the solar system via the Sun after triangulating with a zodiacal sign. Relating this to the energy of the dominant sign gives a very complex picture which we must leave to the study of Esoteric Astrology and Hierarchical releases generally.

The circulation of these energy complexes through the forms in the solar system create the psychic atmosphere in which a planet and all its inhabitants function. In other words, the Planes can be thought of as furnishing the background for the activity of the planet, while the Rays modify the nature of that activity. This background information should make it easier to understand the constant references to the Planes and the Rays in Dwal Khul's teachings.

THE LAW OF CAUSE AND EFFECT

The Law of Cause and Effect is a part of the experience of everyone. If we make a mistake we suffer the consequences or, alternatively, if we perform right action, we enjoy the benefits, in appropriate degrees. This applies to all action. Since we have lived many lives and have made many mistakes (bringing us to the point where we now have some good judgment and the ability to guide our lives with a degree of wisdom), we know the validity of this law.

Inasmuch as the word "Karma" has accumulated a dense cloud of thoughtforms about its meanings, it should be remembered that karma is the law of "cause" and "effect," and therefore relates to all phenomena of any nature. As a Law of Nature, the Law of Cause and Effect covers *all* manifestation, and is the mode of expression of God as far as this planet and the area of our observation is concerned.

All life in the Universe is conditioned by and responds to this law. The smallest movement, the faintest thought, produces causes bringing inevitable effects. Cause and effect are like twin existences clasping each other eternally, seeking that union which is barred by time. The very breath attests to this law of action and reaction. The result of cause, the effect, is bound to that which created it—an integral part, inseparable, eternal, bridging if need be from life to life, from aeon to aeon.

Can this cycle be changed, or are we bound to an endless wheel of cause becoming effect becoming in turn a cause? The wheel may be stopped, its structure broken, but only by a greater cause. And when we know the law, we can make it our servant, and thus build that which the Soul intends. The basic law of evolution, God's Will, is grinding away slowly, yet effects can be changed—the debt may be paid in better coin. This does not deny, but affirms the Law of Karma—a law which if it ceased but for a moment, all things would vanish, for it is the very motion of the primal sparks.

To realize how karma can be offset, it is necessary to see its relationship to the idea of time. To the scientist, time is a steady flow, to be measured in constant intervals, such as the ticks of a clock, or the vibrations of a crystal, or the length of a day, or the rotation of the Earth about the Sun. In other words, time is a standard interval in a continuity, it is a movement from future to past, which does not change and which is applied in some factor of division or multiplication to all events with which scientists are concerned.

Blavatsky defines time as a *sequence of events* or *changes in consciousness*. There is a great deal more said about this in the Secret Doctrine, but not in a form which could be reproduced in this brief explanation of fundamentals. The question is, how does the continuity of action in the past project itself into the future, from one life to another. This future does not exist when the "cause" of an action is recorded or encapsulated in the energy system called "permanent atoms." This "cause" is later reproduced in brain consciousness, triggering effects which seem without explanation. In addition, there are causes external to those recorded in the permanent atoms. They concern the fact that we are part of larger units of consciousness which record the relation we have with other units on our own level and apportion the effects in a given lifespan. These larger units are those on the higher inclusive planes of this Cosmic Physical Plane. Dwal Khul lists this as group, family, national and world karma and the recording and assisting entities as the Lords of Karma.

This "permanent atom" is a very complex unit of energy or an energy system. It exists on the atomic level of each plane and carries with it a complete memory of the past of the entity concerned. This record, showing creative processes both complete and incomplete, is reviewed by in-

telligent entities, the Lords of Karma, in consulta-
tion with the Master and Sponsors concerned with
the individual's welfare and progress, and with his
own Soul (said to be a Master in Its own right).
Finally, a decision is made as to how much of
the incomplete effect, or karma, should be activated in the next life, providing the best opportunities for progress of the Soul and Its
personality.

Returning to the idea of time, Dwal Khul has
said that time does not exist on the mental plane.
He means that time does not exist in the same
terms and according to the same intervals that we
are accustomed to. And yet, as long as there is a
succession of events on the plane of the Soul,
there is an aspect of time. Obviously, it is not the
same aspect. In fact, we can see that there is a
succession of time states and intervals varying
with each higher subplane of our Cosmic
Physical Plane. If we consider the ultimate, the
timespan of the Logos, the events which He takes
note of are at such great intervals that it is said
that "a thousand years is as a day."

Consequently, life as a human being appears
as a very brief flicker, considering that the life of
the Logos is relatively eternal, beginning in a past
so far distant that even astronomical time means
nothing to It and, as far as we know, It will
continue into the future in the same manner.
Understandably, time to the Logos is not the
same as time to us. So, we must approach the
whole matter of time from a different standpoint. Blavatsky uses the word *duration* and

considers time as a series of measure events or changes in consciousness in duration,[1] but the scale of measurement may and does vary. Diagram 6 would seem logical, therefore, to suggest the nature and the fact of duration on the individual.

If the question of duration puzzles you, look at any object. Obviously, it exists in the past; you observe it in the present and usually have no doubt of its existence in the immediate future. Yet, there is no sequence of events; you see this all at once, *in duration*. It cannot exist in the future for the future has not yet arrived. It stands, for the moment, *in the eternal now—duration*.

In this steady sequence of events which constitutes time, we are constantly making decisions, every moment—decisions as to what we shall think, what we allow the emotional elemental to express and what action may come from either one of these aspects producing a future effect, good or bad. It is at this point that we have a *choice* as to where creative activity shall be spent. It is at this point that we make the future. *Whatever you desire the future to be, you must make at this point by your choices, by the decisions that you constantly make as to direction and thought and actions.* If creation is incom-

[1] "'Time' is only an illusion produced by the succession of our states of consciousness as we travel through Eternal Duration, and it does not exist where no consciousness exists in which the illusions can be produced, but 'lies asleep.'" —The Secret Doctrine, Volume II, page 68-69, by H.P. Blavatsky.

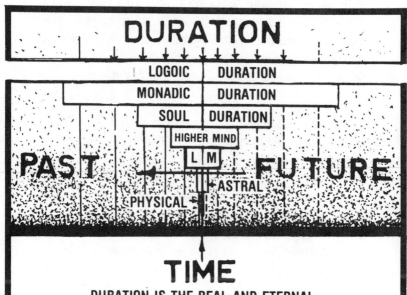

TIME

DURATION IS THE REAL AND ETERNAL.
TIME IS THE MEASURE OF LIMITATION.

'''Time' is only an illusion produced by the succession of our states of consciousness as we travel through eternal duration, and it does not exist where no consciousness exists in which the illusion can be produced, but 'lies asleep.' The present is only a mathematical line which divides that part of eternal duration which we call the future, from that part which we call the past ... these two eternities constitute that duration in which alone anything has true existence, were our senses but able to cognize it.''

Like all things manifested, time is relative to duration. All creation is done in duration, and that is where thoughtforms are built. Therefore, duration is the area where karma may be altered.

DIAGRAM 6

plete in a life, it is carried on into the future and activated for completion when its time arrives. Thus, karma is the completion of a creation started in the past. Remember, the beginning is thought.

Thinking, governed by desire for that which has given pleasure, governs your future. Cease then to be controlled by desire and let your thoughts be directed by that greater identity, the Soul, which controls those events in greater duration than you can encompass. If there are forms of a character that appear undesirable or evil, do not add to them with your small capacity, but add rather to that which is good, beautiful and true. Thus, is the world changed. Thus, you identify with God and aid in the creation of His Kingdom. Thus, you cease to create as the personal-self and become the Soul.

The Ancient Wisdom has defined the process of creation as "White Magic." Put into modern terms by Dwal Khul, "White Magic" is described as a process of observing, choosing, desiring, thinking, vitalizing by desire, and precipitating into the formation of etheric substance, after which physical appearance is inevitable.

We do not say that eliminating bondage from physical limitation is easy, but we do say it is possible. We say with the Master that

> . . . to step definitely and knowingly even but one step on either path (the choice between good and evil) produces *great karmic results.* The mass of men walk waveringly, uncertain as to the goal they aim at; their standard of life is

indefinite; consequently their karma operates in
a confused manner. But when once the threshold of knowledge is reached, the confusion
begins to lessen, and consequently the karmic
results increase enormously, because all are acting in the same direction on all the different
planes; for the occultist cannot be half-hearted,
nor can he return when he has passed the
threshold. These things are as impossible as
that the man should become the child again.
The individuality has approached the state of
responsibility by reason of growth; it cannot
recede from it.
  —The Master Hilarion in <u>Light on the Path</u>
          by Mabel Collins, pages 35-36

Control your own future and your moving present will become what you will and leave nothing
but good. This must be done for you cannot
return to that which you were, and time moves in
one direction only in that creative process which
you can and must control.

We have given this subject more consideration
because of its vast importance. You are beginning the creation of the future in your present
thinking, good or bad. Like any energy, you can
neutralize it by its opposite; but why should you
start wrong? In connection with our work, the
accumulated thoughtforms are all incomplete
creations lacking power to leave your field. A
thoughtform which is propelled with sufficient
energy to leave the field will affect others or the
environment and will produce a different kind of
karma to be worked out in relationships. Those
thoughtforms which are retained in the field and
thus affect the creator can be destroyed by their

maker and the wrongly used creative energy redeemed to build up the Causal field as a reservoir of power for use by the Soul in Its own evolutionary projects. These processes of purification and redemption are given in this book.*

REITERATION

Does a hypothetical person named John Smith die, then enter into some intangible state, to someday enter into another embryonic body and live again in another exciting or weary cycle of activity on this planet? He probably has no memory of such rebirth experience and can discover no evidence in life or memory of any referents as to time, place, name, activity, or death that he can communicate to another. As to his inner nature and response to the new impacts he receives, he may question: Why was he born with abilities that others do not have? Why does he exert himself to succeed in spite of bad environment and unfortunate circumstance generally? Why does he have conscience? From extensions of these and like questions, various

---

*Dwal Khul did not list Karma as an Introductory Postulate, but gave it exhaustive consideration, beginning with THE LIPIKA LORDS or LORDS OF KARMA on page 74 of A Treatise on Cosmic Fire, because it deals with the activity aspect or Third Divine Attribute (an aspect of matter). Because of our emphasis on Techniques we list it as an ACCEPTANCE.

Although the Law of Cause and Effect as we understand it may not be definable on higher levels we have, as with the term consciousness, applied it to all levels of the initiatory-evolutionary processes, leaving more specific and higher application to A Treatise on Cosmic Fire.

conclusions have been drawn both for and against the possibility of such continuity of existence. According to the Ancient Wisdom, reincarnation is a matter of the evolutionary development of the individual; there is continuity of consciousness, but it varies widely, being extremely limited for a vast period of time, and then becoming evident in increasing tempo, until full and constant memory of the past is available to the Master's consciousness. Because of this fact, Dwal Khul uses the term "reiteration" instead of "reincarnation," stating that it appears more suitable since it is not the personality but the Soul that is the incarnating entity, which puts down a portion of itself, yet remains.*

The number 777 is used to suggest the three cycles of incarnations of a decreasing number of lives necessary to make the gains required, thus indicating the time involved between individualization and entrance into "The door of Initiation." The following diagram illustrates this idea.

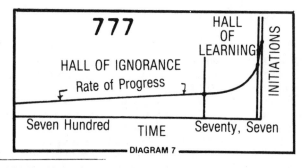

DIAGRAM 7

*The Soul "having pervaded their little universe with a fragment of itself *remains.*"
—Esoteric Astrology, by Alice A. Bailey, p. 618.

In this long series of lives, man first develops instincts which enable him to survive, then the emotional nature to enjoy surviving—or the reverse, then the mental nature to control survival involving both the instincts and the emotions.

Back of these activities there is a constant urge which we call desire, ambition, or aspiration. This pressure is an inner drive as well as response to the attractive energy of the Soul which turns toward itself. It is like the energy which makes plants seek the light, or which makes an animal or man seek comfort, safety and individual betterment of some kind. It is the response of the spark of Divinity at the heart of every atom and form, the God presence which moves under the Law of Attraction toward central unity, a process which we call evolution. There is also an external pull from an entity which is not human at all, although it has been called the True Self or Higher Self, which the Ancient Wisdom calls the *Soul. The Soul is the permanent, reincarnating entity.*

Man cannot be said to reincarnate except as he becomes one with or "fused" with the Soul and his possible recollections of and identification with the past may be in proportion to his fusion with the Soul. There are other factors which interfere with the exact application of this rule, but possibility of better understanding lies in this area. These interfering factors we will consider later under the heading "Phase II— Purification of the Vehicles."

The following diagram is a symbolic outline of the relationship of the Soul to the series of lives in which it seeks to build a vehicle through which *It can function on the physical plane.* The Soul does not work alone but with other Souls as a group. As a group, They guide Their groups of linked animal-men, controlling environment to some extent, making the slow changes in the bodies necessary. In the first long series, the seven hundred, the Souls pay little attention to Their linked animal-men, linked at the time of individualization, but are concerned with the environment and relationships of Their own plane of existence. The link consists objectively (to inner vision) of a tenuous thread of consciousness, a "spark" of Themselves, "put down" and another thread of *life* itself already a part of animal-man.

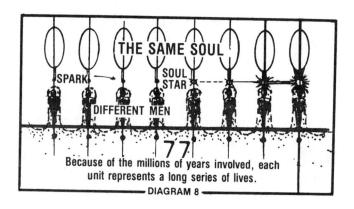

THE SAME SOUL

SPARK

SOUL STAR

DIFFERENT MEN

77

Because of the millions of years involved, each
unit represents a long series of lives.

———— DIAGRAM 8 ————

This diagram symbolizes the period of the seventy-seven, from the entrance into the Hall of Learning to the Probationary Path. Continuity of consciousness between the projected "different men" of Diagram 8 does not begin until late in the cycle and is not fully established until the end of the initiatory cycle. The recall in this continuity is very dim and vague and corresponds to the gained fusion between Soul and personality. The records in the astral light, which are extremely unreliable, are sometimes seen and group records mistaken for personal ones.

There are many types of records of the past and, indeed, all forms are records of the forces which made them. Each man in any incarnation is the sum total of the gains of the past efforts of the Soul to build suitable vehicles, suitable for its full expression. At the end of an incarnation, all personality bodies are successively destroyed, as are the physical brain memories along with the destruction of the cells. The physical vehicle is perpetuated only by the genes in the well-known processes of generation. The subtle vehicles, the astral (emotional) and lower mental bodies are carried forward by the energy systems, called the permanent atoms, which are withdrawn by the Soul and are reenergized during the next downward focus of the Soul. They do *not* carry detailed personality memories, but only the capacities developed.

There is no value in the recall of the details of those immediate past lives which partial fusion with the Soul has made possible. Even if detailed recall were possible, personalities are not able to evaluate such uncertain memories. The essence, which concerns the evolutionary gains intended by the Soul, is extracted at the end of an incarnation and adds to the content of the permanent atoms and the Causal Body of the Soul. Such gains are objectively visible to inner vision and demonstrate as increases in the various colors or energies in the field and Causal Body, and which grow more intense as time passes. If the disciple wishes to know past lives he will find such information in identification with the Soul, but when he reaches that capacity he will probably not be interested.

There is a type of recall which concerns the elimination of the hindering thoughtforms that form a dense cloud about all disciples who have not consciously destroyed them. We shall say more about this under the heading of "Purification of the Vehicles."

Thus concludes our brief comments on reincarnation, adding to what we have said under a description of the Acceptances, "Reincarnation is a Fact."

INITIATION — ENFORCED EVOLUTION

The first comment which should be made about initiation is that it is an *abnormal process*. It is an experiment which has been tried on three planets. It has proved to be a success on one, is proving successful on Earth, and undoubtedly will be successful on the third planet as well.* If initiation is an abnormal process, what then is

---

*Initiation Human and Solar, by Alice A. Bailey, p. 96.

the normal process? The fact is that humanity would evolve without initiation, or the process of stimulated or enforced evolution. There is a spark of divinity which follows the great cycles through the Will of God Himself, built into the very atoms of our being. It is inevitable that all humanity will, in the end, follow the Path of Return.

In A Treatise on Cosmic Fire, page 373, there is a very complicated diagram showing a great series of planetary manifestations. The diagram indicates a series of events or positions in which the units have moved downward into dense matter and then, after passing the deepest point, moved upward toward spirit. The smallest unit at the deepest point represents our planet Earth. The following diagram on page 385 of Cosmic Fire depicts the lowest group or "scheme," again magnified, with Earth at the deepest point. If this point were to be magnified further, Earth would again be at the lowest point. This indicates that the *passing of the Earth through the lowest point is also the turning point for the vaster manifestations successively.* This may be a reason why this small planet has the distinction of having its evolutionary processes speeded up by the Will of the Planetary Logos.

Humanity, having self-consciousness, is the first of the kingdoms to have the creative power of mind, and it is at this point that the pressure and opportunity to shorten the evolutionary process is applied. The techniques of enforced evolution used require the assistance of the kingdoms above the human, and most of all from the next kingdom, the Kingdom of Soul, the Planetary Hierarchy. *This speeding up process is called Initiation.*

Let us consider more specifically what this process of enforced evolution is. The word "enforced" has been questioned somewhat, because the Soul does not force, but works through persuasion. However, the forcing, if that term may be used, is not on the part of the Soul. The Soul offers an opportunity, but does not interfere with evolution. The opportunity offered by the Soul is a stimulation of the normal aspiration and urge to betterment. Enforced evolution is the Soul's response to the efforts of the personal self to link with and carry out Its program, which is an ultimate merging with It in which the personality is absorbed by the Soul.

Although Dwal Khul speaks of the initiations as "enforced evolution," since the Soul works by persuasion, it has been suggested that "stimulated evolution" might be more descriptive. The intiations are not simple affairs and the book Initiation, Human and Solar[1] gives much in the way of detail.

In Externalization of the Hierarchy, page 17, Dwal Khul says:

---

[1]All students should study the two books referred to herein, the first by Alice A. Bailey called From Bethlehem to Calvary or the Initiations of Jesus, and the second by Dwal Khul called Initiation, Human and Solar. If students follow the techniques herein given, they will accomplish the clearing without such study, but in the end they must know what is said in these books.

. . . Men and women have offered themselves
for intellectual training and have subjected
themselves to a *forcing process* which is intended to bring the full power of the Soul into
premature blossoming, and this in order more
rapidly and effectively to serve the race, and to
cooperate with the plan of the Hierarchy. Such
students thereby leave themselves open to
dangers and difficulties which would have been
avoided had they chosen to go the slower and
equally sure way. . . . He should not be permitted to be afraid or to refuse to subject himself
to this forcing process, but he should enter
upon it with his eyes wide open and he should
be taught to avail himself of the safeguards offered and the experience of older students.*

From the standpoint of the Occidental world,
the life of Jesus of Nazareth is an outstanding
example of how a life of spirituality can affect a
whole planet. An examination of the details of
His life reveals a number of incidents which were
so outstanding that they have become a structure
of belief and teaching wherever the so-called
Christian world is dominant. In her book
From Bethlehem to Calvary, Alice A. Bailey
described these incidents as The Initiations of
Jesus. Jesus had taken the First, Second and
Third Initiations in previous lives. He recapi-
tulated these in the episodes called Birth,
Baptism and Transfiguration. The Fourth Initia-
tion was literally His Crucifixion and death. The
Fifth Initiation He took as Apollonius of Tyana.

All initiations must be taken as an incarnated

*Emphasis added.

Soul on the Physical plane. Each initiation is a raising in vibration to a point which cannot be maintained at first, but the disciple learns to handle this higher vibration before the next initiation. Although the Third Initiation usually causes death to the vehicles, it is a project of Hierarchy at this time to maintain the incarnation beyond the Third Initiation if possible because of the need for physical plane teachers. Thus, in the past, the lesser initiations were likely to be taken at the beginning of a life. and the Third Initiation at the end of the life.

The intiations are listed below:

1. *Birth*   *Threshold Initiation*
2. *Baptism*   *Threshold Initiation*
3. *Transfiguration* *First Cosmic Initiation*
4. *Crucifixion*   *Second Cosmic Initiation*
5. *Resurrection*   *Third Cosmic Initiation*

These are the Biblical names; the occult names of the Fourth and Fifth Cosmic Initiations are Renunciation and Revelation, respectively.

In the past, it has been assumed that the initiations were solely a concern of the churches and/or occult or philosophical groups. The truth is that the initiations concern those individuals qualified by their development, in *all departments of human activity*. Dwal Khul lists, in Discipleship in the New Age, Volume I, pages 35-40, the different categories and departments of human activity wherein disciple-initiates function:

1. Telepathic Communicators;
2. Trained Observers;
3. Magnetic Healers;
4. Educators of the New Age;
5. Political Organizers;
6. Workers in the Field of Religion;
7. Scientific Servers;
8. Psychologists;
9. Financiers and Economists;
10. Creative Workers.

Many disciple-initiates working in these various areas mentioned may never have heard of the initiatory process or the Planetary Hierarchy, or perhaps any of the Acceptances, but they do have much in common. Dwal Khul has described how to recognize First and Second Degree initiates in the book The Rays and the Initiations, page 667:

> Members of the New Group of World Servers should watch with care for all those who show signs of having passed through the 'birth' experience and should help them toward a greater maturity. They should assume that all those who truly love their fellow men, who are interested in esoteric teaching, and who seek to discipline themselves in order to attain greater beauty of life, are initiate and have undergone the First Initiation. When they discover those who are seeking mental polarization and who evidence a desire and aspiration to think and to know, coupled with the distinguishing marks of those who have taken the First Initiation, they can, in all probability, safely asume that such people have taken the Second Initiation or are on the verge of so doing. Their duty will then be

clear. It is by this close observation on the part
of the World Servers that the ranks of the New
Group are filled. Today, the opportunity and
the stimulation are so great that all servers must
keep alert, developing in themselves the ability
to register the quality for which search must be
made, and giving the help and guidance which
will weld into one cooperative band those
disciples and initiates who should prepare the
way for the Christ.

It may be asked, if these disciples are First and
Second Degree Initiates and the initiations must
be taken on the physical plane as incarnated
Souls, why don't they remember something of
the experience? It is said that the initiations are
taken either at the beginning of a life, before
patterns have formed or activated, or at the end
of a life when the effect on the vehicles is unimportant. If the initiation is taken at the beginning
of the life or close to it, it is very easy for the
child, who may have very little brain development, to assume that the experience was
imaginary or to forget it entirely as the more
interesting episodes of personality life unfold.
The early years of an incarnation are generally
characterized by intense involvement in everything which the senses perceive, and the child,
not understanding the experience, may have put
it below the threshold of conscious memory, for
later recall. Both authors recall these experiences
which occurred at the ages of five and seven.

The initiations are recognitions of completions
in a process of compressing normal or slow
evolution tremendously in time. These recognitions by Hierarchy are ceremonies in the lower

degrees but take different forms in the higher degrees.

The steps of evolution, leading to the initiatory process, whether normal or stimulated, follow the Path of Return from consciousness manifesting in densest matter in the long ladder of evolution toward higher and more rarified forms, toward a more inclusive manifestation of spirit, toward higher and more inclusive forms and, in the end, toward the consciousness of God Himself. We do not lose our individuality in this process. If, for example, we choose to focus our attention on that which we have been, it can be recalled to any degree of vividness that we desire. It is in this sense that we can go back in time. The obvious comment that such a return would be an illusion can be countered by calling attention to the fact that what we consider as our present reality and form in time and space is also an illusion.

Since, ". . . *all in nature will be, is, or has been through the human kingdom,*" quoting Dwal Khul in A Treatise on Cosmic Fire, page 1030, it is apparent that the course of evolutionary growth is not confined to this planet. This rather startling statement means that humanity is only one of the steps or stages between the lowest and the highest, between what we consider dense matter and spirit, between the densest manifestation in the cosmos and the ultimate galaxy, or quasar, or black hole, or whatever form the spirit-matter combination may take in the infinite space around us. *It intimately relates us*

*to all manifestations and all kingdoms on this
planet.* Since all is life, and manifestation of life,
and all forms carry the spiritual essence with
them, it means that *all things, all manifestations,
are brothers.*

In normal evolution, much of what we consider as dangers producing difficulties and tensions do not appear, because the growth and
changes are so slow that consciousness adapts
itself more easily, without the strains, tensions,
and dangers which the forcing or stimulated
process produces.

Keeping in mind that as it is below, so it is
above, we confine our attention to that area in
which our consciousness functions and which is
only a portion of the Cosmic Physical Plane. It is
in relation to these planes and subplanes of the
Cosmic Physical Plane that the processes of
initiation take place.

The initiations are a process of gradually re-
fining and raising the vibration and frequency of
the personality vehicles in order to liberate the
Soul. Dwal Khul has stated in A Treatise on the
Seven Rays, Volume Two, page 51:

> It might be said that the liberation of the Soul
> or Ego comes about when its work of salvaging
> matter (through utilizing it and building it into
> forms) has been carried forward to a desired
> point. It is not primarily due to the attainment
> of a certain spiritual stature by the man and the
> demonstration of certain spiritual qualities.
> This desired stature and these spiritual qualities

are manifested when the vehicles have been 'occultly saved,' and matter has thus been transformed, transmuted and symbolically 'raised up into heaven.' When the vehicles vibrate in unison with the Soul, then is liberation achieved.

We have emphasized that whether the evolutionary process is normal or enforced, the effect on the vehicles is *change* or, as the quotation says, the matter of the vehicles is raised.

This raising process continues steadily and, we are told, that by the Second Initiation twenty-five percent of the atoms of the vehicles have been raised to the atomic level, and therefore more directly responsive to the Monad or Spirit. By the Third Initiation fifty percent have been so raised. This would imply that by the Fourth Initiation seventy-five percent of the atoms of the vehicles would be changed and that the change would be completed at the time of the Fifth Initiation. However, this is not exactly so, because after the Third Initiation the processes involved are speeded up; the halfway point has been passed and the infusion process, or the process by which the personality is absorbed by the Soul, has progressed to the point where the Soul is in control and the objective is to complete the initiatory process as quickly as possible.

There is another example which occurs, which has not been emphasized but is just as important, and that is the change in the nadis, or threads, which compose the etheric body. In the beginning, there are five strands, but in the end only two are left. There are also changes in the system of etheric centers, a process which begins at the First Initiation when the heart center is stimulated by the Christ. At the Second Initiation, other major centers are stimulated and after the Third Initiation, when the disciple has been accepted as a conscious member of Hierarchy, the kundalini fire is raised in its fullness, and complete control of the major and minor centers is established by the disciple-initiate.

In summing up this section on Initiation, we realize that we may be speaking to students who know nothing of the subject. Also, the reality of the subjective worlds, types of intelligences and individual consciousnesses such as Souls, Spirits and the like, has not been generally accepted in the past by many thinkers. At the present time, science and some other groups have come to the place where they are compelled to consider, tentatively at least, that this is a field of investigation which has been neglected.

It should be remembered that the goal of the Planetary Logos is for humanity as a whole to take the First Initiation. The building of the Antahkarana enables the energies of the Planetary Logos to be brought down to Earth. We cannot overemphasize the importance of this work and its value to the Externalization forces of Hierarchy, for, without the cooperation of incarnated disciples, the Kingdom of Heaven cannot be brought to Earth nor can the Christ return to complete His work.

CHAPTER IV

EXTERNALIZATION

PROGRAM OF THE CHRIST

*"Thy Kingdom come . . .
on Earth as it is in Heaven."*
—The Lord's Prayer

Has it not been forgotten that the objective of
the Great Teacher was to bring the Kingdom of
Heaven to Earth and that, in order to do this, He
gave the principles which must govern human
relationships in the simple invocation: *Peace on
Earth, goodwill among men*? And is it not
evident that such progress as humanity has made
has been in proportion to the implementation of
this invocation? This invocation is to become a
command as the *sword* of the Spiritual Will
governs mankind when wielded by the hand of
the Returning Teacher. Thus will the Aquarian

Age become manifest.

The Planetary Hierarchy, as the spiritual government of the planet, is ready and joyous in its response to the long-awaited demand of humanity for honest leadership and freedom from conflict. It might be asked why the Great Ones have not intervened to prevent the ominous development which threatens the destruction of all that we have built and gained in the past. Because this planet is like a school, and the method of learning is the trial-and-error process which establishes right direction. The teachings of Hierarchy, and the Law of Cause and Effect, give all the guidance permitted by the Logos. The right reactions of humanity are the evidences that the lessons are learned.

It is at this time, when the cry of humanity touches Hierarchy, that it becomes possible for Hierarchy to move closer, into conscious contact and communication, which represents a descent into a denser and more difficult vibration for Them. Like individual men who seek to become Soul infused, humanity invokes the Soul of the planet, Hierarchy, and invites the greater infusion. Broadly speaking, this descent into matter of the Kingdom of Heaven (as Hierarchy has been called) is what is meant by the term "Externalization of the Hierarchy."

Now, near the end of this century, we are at the high point of a dying culture. Call it what you will, the evidence of failure is upon us—a failure to establish right human relationships as the foundation upon which a permanent economic and social structure can be raised and maintained. Leadership is false or lacking. The unthinking multitude is being forced to think as a result of fading freedoms, and the deeper thinkers are probing to uncover the ideas and the ideals upon which the New and Dawning Age must be built. The quality of leadership which has brought us to this desperate situation is being urgently examined, and an invocation for honest government is growing among the thinkers of humanity today. Is this a vain hope or possibility, or perhaps a guarantee for the future? It is said that when the invocative cry of humanity reaches a certain crescendo, the gods respond and use that accumulated energy of invocation to precipitate that which is demanded.

Thus, the word "externalization" refers to the response of the next higher kingdom, the Kingdom of Souls, to a cry of distress by humanity, and Their decision to function openly among humanity once more, after the long withdrawal which followed the destruction of Atlantis.

Something of the message of the Christ, that He would return sometime in the future to complete His mission, is recognized by almost everyone. The idea of the Returning Saviour is even broader, because almost all religions expect the manifestation of a Divine and Spiritual Teacher who will solve the problems of the world and inaugurate a New Age, or that period in which right and spiritual relationships are the goal and accomplishment of humanity.

Relatively few recognize that the phrase "Externalization of the Hierarchy" refers to the Return of the Christ. It should not appear strange that much more is involved than just the appearance of One who is historically known as a spiritual teacher. A little thought will bring to recognition the fact that the Christ had a number of close followers who have, in those intervening centuries, progressed under His teaching to the place where they are quite competent to work with Him on the problems of humanity today.

In the past, a single teacher incarnated to present a new and more suitable teaching for the keynote of the New Age. In the case of the Buddha, He drew around Him nine hundred Arhats, or Fourth Degree Initiates, who spread the teaching after His withdrawal. It is said that the Christ will require nine thousand Arhats before He can return—this being a prerequisite established by the Planetary Logos. In addition to these Arhats, the incarnation of millions of lesser disciples and initiates makes an invincible army.

At the beginning of the Christ's spiritual mission, two thousand years ago, there had been a few "forerunners," the most outstanding of whom was John the Baptist. At the present time, preparations for the Return of the Christ are more extensive, because of the fact that Hierarchy Itself will descend, with the Christ as Its leader.

In the two thousand year period since the beginning of His mission, the Christ has stimulated and brought many to initiation, most of whom have become a part of that intermediate group between Hierarchy and humanity called by Dwal Khul the New Group of World Servers.

In the early 1930's Dwal Khul focused His attention on this New Group of World Servers and the meditations of that decade were intended to prevent the spiritual conflict on the mental levels from precipitating on the physical plane. But, as Dwal Khul said, there were not enough spiritually-minded disciples and humanity chose to fight it out on the physical plane thus insuring, as He said, that the Christ would appear in physical manifestation.

The Master Morya, quoted by Helena Roerich, has stated that Armageddon began in 1932. It is obvious, fifty years later, that the crisis of Armageddon is *now*.

The idea of battle or conflict has been avoided by cults of affirmation and denial. The Christian Science philosophy from which many such groups come was based upon a false assumption, as stated in their Scientific Statement of Being, "There is no Life, Truth, Intelligence, or substance in matter . . ." thus, denying the basic involutionary appearance of God as spirit-matter, each dependent upon the other as the Divine basis of all creation. Spirit-matter and their relationship—consciousness—manifests in three fundamental qualities:

Rajas   —   *Activity*
Sattva   —   *Balance or Harmony*
Tamas   —   *Inertia*

In time and space there is a cyclic imbalance in which intelligence, in form on some level, ensoul those qualities and it is in the cyclic imbalance that those conflicts arise which may be good or evil to lesser entities, but which cyclically lead to balance and harmony. It is the stimulus of these extremes and the production of harmony and balance which causes each successive period to be on a higher turn of the time spiral. This is all part of the emerging Plan implementing an unknown purpose of God.

The New Age or Aquarian Age is to be a demonstration of balance and harmony. Early in this century it was not certain in Hierarchy when the turning point from Kali Yuga (Dark Age) to the light of Aquarius would take place. However, in 1942 the turning point did take place. Disciples in the Arcane School and Dwal Khul's group were told that humanity had failed and that the destruction of civilization was again contemplated. However, the cry of humanity for peace grew to a point where the energies reached beyond this planet, and Cosmic Entities took note and instituted action to end the war. Since that time progress has been rapid and the chaotic condition now in evidence is the climax. Because of the crystallized condition of the old and its opposition to change, such climaxes occur at the end of every age.

The Battle of Armageddon is a symbolic name for the conflict which always occurs at the end of an age. In a minor age termination, as at present, it may be only a short period of chaos and destruction, but at the end of a greater age it may lead to complete obliteration of the planet on physical levels. Such conflict and destruction of old systems and values clear the path for the advent of the Light of the New Age, thus, it could be called Externalization or Manifestation of the Light of descending Hierarchy.

The goal of externalization is not so much to enable individuals to reach a heavenly state of consciousness as it is to *bring it to Earth:* It is not enough to think and meditate about this transformation. It is up to the aspirants and disciples of the world to make practical application of what they know through climbing the ladder of evolution in consciousness and to apply the principles of the Aquarian Age. In so doing, disciples will change all of the ten departments of human activity, civilization and culture into something which cannot be anticipated or visualized at the present time. The work proposed is to hasten the day—"to shorten the days without which no flesh shall live." *This will be a sufficient goal for those who respond.* May the increasing tensions of the changeover to the New Age of Aquarius be transmuted into right action, feeling and thought by the Children of the Dawn.

We, the authors of the <u>Rainbow Bridge</u> series, have worked on some phase of the Externaliza-

tion Program for most of this century. Our
books emphasize techniques which tell disciples
how to prepare the vehicles for the impact of the
energies of the Changeover from the Piscean to
the Aquarian Age and particularly to become
channels for the grounding of higher energies
which they could not otherwise endure. This is in
line with Dwal Khul's statement that "Hierarchy
cannot function on the physical plane except
through incarnated disciples."[1] Because of the
great need at this time of crisis even a small
contribution on the physical plane may be the
basis of great expansions of Hierarchy. As Dwal
Khul has said, "It is a time of great
opportunity."

THE NEW GROUP OF WORLD SERVERS

Dwal Khul has emphasized that the true
critical experience of the Christ was not at the
time of the crucifixion, which related to the
Master Jesus, but occurred when the over-
shadowing Christ was in the Garden of Gethsemane.

In the silence of the Garden, the Christ sat
alone, against the curtain of the dark future
unrolled before Him. The "Kingdom of
Heaven" awaited Him. He knew He had but to
turn to the Light. For Him there was no more

[1]The Master Dwal Khul had thought that the subject of Externalization of the Hierarchy was important enough to require a
book by that title and also The Reappearance of the Christ.

death. For Him awaited the Kingdom, the Power and the Glory. The reality He had earned; the angels were silent and waiting.

It is at this critical point that the Christ decided to stay on Earth and follow the Path of Earth Service. He saw His mission before Him, the future of humanity, the Souls in Hell, the Hell of darkness, the Hell of the unreal, of disease and death. Symbolically, He descended into Hell for three days—three thousand years—to teach the Souls there. This was His mission, to turn His back upon the Heaven World that He had earned and focus His attention on bringing Light and Love and Power to this darkened planet.

Ever since the experience in the Garden of Gethsemane, the Christ has been searching for those among humanity in whom the spark of Soul responded, and who could be stimulated and brought to the point of development where they could take the First and Second Initiations.

This army of disciples has been growing during the last two thousand years under the guidance and direction of the Christ in preparation for the time when He will reappear among men, this time with the symbolic sword of Will and Power. This group of forerunners was a part of the deliberate plan of the Planetary Hierarchy to implement and make the necessary changes in the consciousness of humanity enabling the Christ to return.

This group of disciples has been coming into incarnation in rapidly increasing numbers. The number has grown from a few hundred on the planet to millions. They are not an organization, yet are bound by common atttudes and convictions. They are oriented toward service and group activities, and are scattered among all departments of human activity. They are to be found in all races and groups of any consequence, and as they mature they will make changes for the better wherever they are to be found. In general they rebel against customs, codes and conventions, observing the older generation's failure to live up to them, and are aware of the disastrous condition of human affairs everywhere. Many of the qualities they have will not be recognized until circumstances force them, in this chaotic period of the Changeover, to step forward and outline the basic ideas of right human relationships and take positions of leadership and guidance. Then they will apply their own principles of right human relationships wherever they are and in whatever type of activity they find themselves. *These individuals form the group which has been called the New Group of World Servers.*

Even if unconscious of status, and not working directly and intelligently on some world problem, all members of this group are transmitters of energy, the quality and direction of which is conditioned by individual development. This fact, and the attitude they hold toward their environment, causes these disciples to be a force for those changes which will bring in the New Age. If students work conscientiously and consciously, they become a *power*.

The apparent dismal and disintegrating condition of human institutions and the many conflicts of today are the result of evolutionary processes. Cyclically, natural law would take effect, and the civilizations and cultures would come to an end and rebuild on a higher turn of the evolutionary spiral taking what we would consider to be great periods of geological time. At this time, however, the Planetary Hierarchy is intervening to prevent a setback in evolutionary time. This is only possible because of the advent of the New Group of World Servers who act as *intermediaries* between Hierarchy and Humanity, by stepping down the energies released. In the days immediately ahead, the Christ will wield the Sword of Divine Will, tempered by Spiritual Will. This conditioned energy must be handled by the New Group of World Servers, who step down and adapt this energy for humanity.

Hierarchy

Communicators   Organized Observers

New Group of
World Servers
Humanity

Thus, the New Group of World Servers is to function as an intermediate group between Humanity and Hierarchy, partaking of both. In a sense, they make a sacrifice that all intermediate groups make in order to provide the necessary vehicles for the implementation of the energies of the New Age.

Since the culture and civilization of any time has generally been the result of the efforts of very few individuals in all departments of human activity, what then can we expect when a large number of qualified individuals take part, and take over as they will do? The result will be nothing less than the long prayed for New Age, sometimes defined as the Millenium, thus indicating a cycle and a higher state of development. Many of these disciples are "standing in the wings" ready to step forward with ideals, guidance and leadership that they may bring order out of the present chaotic period of the Changeover. These individuals will play an important part in bringing about a new world order, and a cycle of a different kind will have its permanent effect resulting in a cultural change beyond present recognition.

The simple techniques in this book enable disciples to link with Hierarchy, and with the Christ, and with the Logos, and the planet itself in a constructive way in this period of Changeover. Not only is this necessary for the planet, but each disciple represents another channel of energy, lightening the planet, thus, coming closer and closer to the point where the Christ can reappear openly. The time when this can happen depends upon the awakening of the New Group of World Servers.

This is the project that we have successfully followed all our lives, consequently, it falls upon us to accelerate that progress at this time and try to spread the teaching of the Ancient Wisdom in such a way that disciples will come into recognition of their own status soon enough to minimize the suffering of mass consciousness. Any gain at all in the direction of this linkage and the weaving of the thread, or the bridge or the Antahkarana for the planet as a whole, will save days of real suffering for humanity. We face that period and are trying to mitigate the serious consequences as far as we can in those years remaining. This is our main objective in calling attention to the very real existence of a group of people scattered all over the planet, not an organization but an organism, which has lightened the whole planet and which has the capacity to take over in all departments and rid the planet of the many evils which have come to the surface at this time for their final destruction.

CHAPTER V

PHASE I — LINK WITH THE SOUL

"Students would do well . . . to pay more attention to the recognition of that in them which 'having prevaded their little universe with a fragment of itself REMAINS.'"

—Esoteric Astrology, page 618

TECHNIQUES IN GENERAL

The real purpose of our work lies in this section concerning techniques and the implementation of these techniques by disciples of the First and Second Degrees. We have described the characteristics which identify them and there are so many of these new disciples now that it is probable that those interested in books of this nature are such First and Second Degree

Initiates.*

The techniques given in this book have been divided into two phases:

PHASE I, LINK WITH THE SOUL

We have repeated the first phase techniques, which were originally published in 1975, because it is most necessary that the work of the first phase, that of building the Central Channel, be completed before undertaking the more difficult work of purification contained in Phase II.

PHASE II, THE SCIENCE OF PURIFICATION

The techniques we have developed have been tried and proven effective, and yet are quite different from the aspirational methods of the past. However, the requirements of externalization are distinctly designed to produce effects on the physical plane.

Our emphasis on techniques may not please those who have a mystical idea of what the Aquarian Age will bring. But, it should be remembered that ideas about the Aquarian Age have generally been filtered through the mystics of the Piscean Age. Consequently, an emphasis upon aspiration and devotion and the building of character have colored practically all of the older quotations of the Ancient Wisdom.

The Aquarian Age is essentially *practical* and its real beginning is the Externalization of the

---

*Dwal Khul's definition of First and Second Degree Initiates appears in this book under the heading, "Initiation—Enforced Evolution," and in The Rays and Initiations, by Alice A. Bailey, page 667.

Planetary Hierarchy and the Return of the Christ.
In other words, the Aquarian Age will materialize
the mystical objectives of the Piscean Age as well
as change the focus of consciousness from the
emotional nature to the concrete mind and,
finally, to that of the Soul. Because the approach
must be practical, it is evident that disciples must
be instructed as to what to do on the physical
plane in terms of those changes which will enable
the New Group of World Servers to make
positive preparation for the Third Initiation, as
well as to make themselves an intermediate
kingdom between Hierarchy and Humanity, thus
becoming transmitters and implementers of the
Plan. We add here the obvious conclusion that to
function on the physical plane the energies of
matter and substance must be used by Hierarchy
and not left to their misuse by the Brothers of
Darkness.[†]

The Piscean Age emphasized heaven as an
objective above and beyond life on Earth. Consequently, disciples sought by all possible means
to reach and enter into that ideal state which they
called the Kingdom of Heaven. In the Piscean
Age, the Return of the Christ was a remote
objective only to occur when Earth itself came to
an end. The human body was a sinful obstacle to
be ignored or punished, and all that pleased it
was the work of the Devil. There was no real or
tangible sense of what the Return of the Christ

[†]". . . the Hierarchy need not be further handicapped by
working in substance whilst the Forces of Evil work both in
substance and in matter."
—Externalization of the Hierarchy, page 689.

meant.

However, the Aquarian Age has a different objective. Earth itself must be changed and moved forward in its evolution so that a more suitable environment and opportunity can be provided for the evolution of the kingdoms of Earth. This change must be made by humanity, a humanity inspired and led by the Christ and His Church (His disciples who have recognized and worked with Him).

Our techniques are designed to make those changes in the vehicles which will enable the energies of the Aquarian Age to be brought down to Earth through these disciples mentioned. The techniques are the result of a step-by-step process of dealing with appearances and conditions which are as objective to us, because of clairvoyant vision, as a carpenter's tools and materials are to him. Because we could observe the changes which took place during our experiments, we were able to take voluminous notes describing what happened when different phrases or words were used. We were also able to see what did not work, and could rule out many practices which had become almost standard forms of meditation. Therefore, the methods evolved gradually through observation and experiment and a discarding of that which did not produce favorable results.

The esoteric history of this planet points out that for each step forward in the evolutionary development of humanity, a way of stimulating that development and making the next step easier has been presented by the Teachers of the race, the Planetary Hierarchy. These steps have been called "yogas" and the following tabulation outlines their relationship to the main racial divisions called the Root Races, which correspond to the development of humanity at that particular time:

Root Race	Racial Name	Yoga	Focus
Third Root Race	Lemuria	Hatha	Physical
Fourth Root Race	Atlantis	Bhakti	Astral/ Emotional
Fifth Root Race	Aryan	Raja	Mind
Sixth Root Race	Age of Aquarius	Agni	Higher Mind/Soul

These yogas were adapted to suit the development of humanity of the particular Root Race. During the Lemurian period, the Third Root Race, the vehicles of humanity were scarcely more developed than animals, being very coarse-textured and insensitive. Accordingly, Hatha Yoga focused on extreme elements of pleasure and pain in order to bring awareness down to the physical plane. These physical extremes of Hatha Yoga are entirely unsuited to the sensitive vehicles of today's disciples.

If you accept the statement that 18 million years have passed since the time of individualization, you can recognize that great changes have been made during that time. It is said that the latest method, or yoga, includes all prior experiments, but this is not a literal injunction to adopt or even to use those outworn methods of the past.

For disciples who have had many incarnations, the older techniques are below the threshold of consciousness and do not need to be revived. In fact, it would be detrimental to bring them up from the depths of the past, since they interfere with the complete and more suitable yogas of the present.

For humanity as a whole, the Kingly or Raja Yoga, as described in the Yoga Sutras of Patanjali, presents the mental approach. For disciple-initiates, we could begin to add something of the Agni Yoga approach, emphasized by the Master Morya in a series of books dictated to Helena Roerich.[‡] The books of the Master Dwal Khul, as a whole, combine the best and most suitable of all the developments of the past.

To attain the objectives of Raja Yoga, Dwal Khul has said:

> The work required is twofold:
>
> 1. To teach them (individuals) how to link up the personal lower self with the over-shadowing Soul so that in the physical brain there is an assured consciousness as to the reality of that divine fact. This knowledge renders the hitherto assumed reality of the three worlds futile to attract and hold, and is the first step, out of the fourth, into the fifth kingdom.
>
> 2. To give such practical instruction as will enable the aspirant to

[‡]The series of books dictated to Helena Roerich by the Master Morya may be obtained from the Agni Yoga Society, 319 West 107th Street, New York, N.Y. 10025.

a. Understand his own nature. This involves some knowledge of the teaching of the past as to the constitution of man and an appreciation of the interpretations of modern Eastern and Western investigators.

b. Control the forces of his own nature and learn something of the forces with which he is surrounded.

c. Enable him so to unfold his latent powers that he can deal with his own specific problems, stand on his own feet, handle his own life, solve his own difficulties and become so strong and poised in spirit that he forces recognition of his fitness as a white magician, and as one of that band of consecrated disciples whom we call the "hierarchy of our planet."[§]

Although our techniques are form-oriented, they are designed to achieve the above ends. The words "form" and "formless" are used in relation to the lower and higher mind, but this is a relative term because wherever there is consciousness there is form of a degree and density appropriate to the level on which it is functioning. Therefore, to be "form-oriented" is not necessarily an indication of being on the "left-hand path." Even a superficial study of Dwal Khul's books should reveal that the purification and raising or redeeming of the matter of the personality vehicles is one of the main objectives and necessities of esoteric techniques.

We do not claim that our methods are final.

§A Treatise on White Magic, by Alice A. Bailey, pages 55-56.

Undoubtedly, sometime in the future, methods which involve a more specific use of color and sound will improve what we have accomplished so far. However, what we do claim is that the techniques described more fully in the following chapters, evolved from our personal experiences and observations, *will* make the changes in the vehicles as described. Our work has been successful and approved by Hierarchy.

PRELIMINARY REMARKS TO PHASE I

Because of our clairvoyant vision we were able to detect certain indications of development in the magnetic auras of initiates. We noticed the existence of a band or thread of light and energy which passed through a sun-like center six inches above the head, upward into space and downward into Earth.

Because of the type and appearance of the energy flow along this thread, distinguishable when it was enlarged to a certain dimension, it has been called the Rainbow Bridge. This thread is a symbolic "bridge" in consciousness between the highest aspect of the personality (the concrete mind) and the lowest aspect of the Soul (the abstract mind).

The Rainbow Bridge, or Antahkarana as it has been called, is referred to in countless ways throughout the works of Dwal Khul as the sutratma or the sushumna, the latter referring to the lowest thread, corresponding to the physical nerve and the sutratma corresponding to the completed bridge.* It is also the vertical arm of the three crosses of occult recognition: The Cardinal, Fixed and Mutable Crosses. Dwal Khul has described the Antahkarana as "'a line, emerging from the earth and ending in the ocean' —referring to the sutratma which, when the antahkarana is completed, blends all types of consciousness, spirit and matter, into one living whole, the ultimate Reality."†

The appearance of the Antahkarana has been indicated pictorially, diagrammatically and symbolically in the various diagrams and plates of this book. It is this thread or band and its expansion, use and value to the individual and his contribution to Humanity and Hierarchy, which is one of the most important subjects of this book.

The statement has been made that, "If students will use the Soul Mantram, build the Central Channel and use the cleansing vortex, and become anchor points of Hierarchy, and transmitters of needed energies, they will aid greatly in the externalizing process." Our purpose is much more than personal assistance, however. *There is a desperate need at this time for disciples to make this first link of building the bridge to the Soul and Hierarchy, for it enables disciples to become channels for the transmission*

---

*More detailed information on this subject can be found in Dwal Khul's books, Education in the New Age, and The Rays and Initiations, by Alice A. Bailey.

†Discipleship in the New Age, Volume II, by Alice A. Bailey, page 266.

of energies so urgently needed by the Christ and His Masters for the coming Externalization of the Planetary Hierarchy. Such aspiring students can be of vital use to the Hierarchy from the very start of their work, which will enable them to take part in this final period of the Changeover from the Piscean to the Aquarian Age. The energies which can be invoked and evoked, and transmitted into the etheric network of the planet will enable the Christ and His disciples to *shorten* the days of suffering threatening to overwhelm the planet.

We close this preliminary statement with the Master Morya's beautiful words as to the bridge of which the Central Channel is a manifestation and a beginning. This bridge will be the present theme of all our efforts, and we urge you to build this bridge as the Brothers of Light and the Christ have done. Become a part of the bridge between Heaven and Earth, between the present age and the new, between that which you appear to be and the Shining One which is your Soul. Only thus can the Externalization of the Hierarchy and the Return of the Christ be possible.

THE TECHNIQUES OF PHASE I—
LINK WITH THE SOUL

In the past we have accepted students and given material only to those whom we could contact personally and verify the indications from the use of a questionnaire and from clairvoyant observation that they could do the work

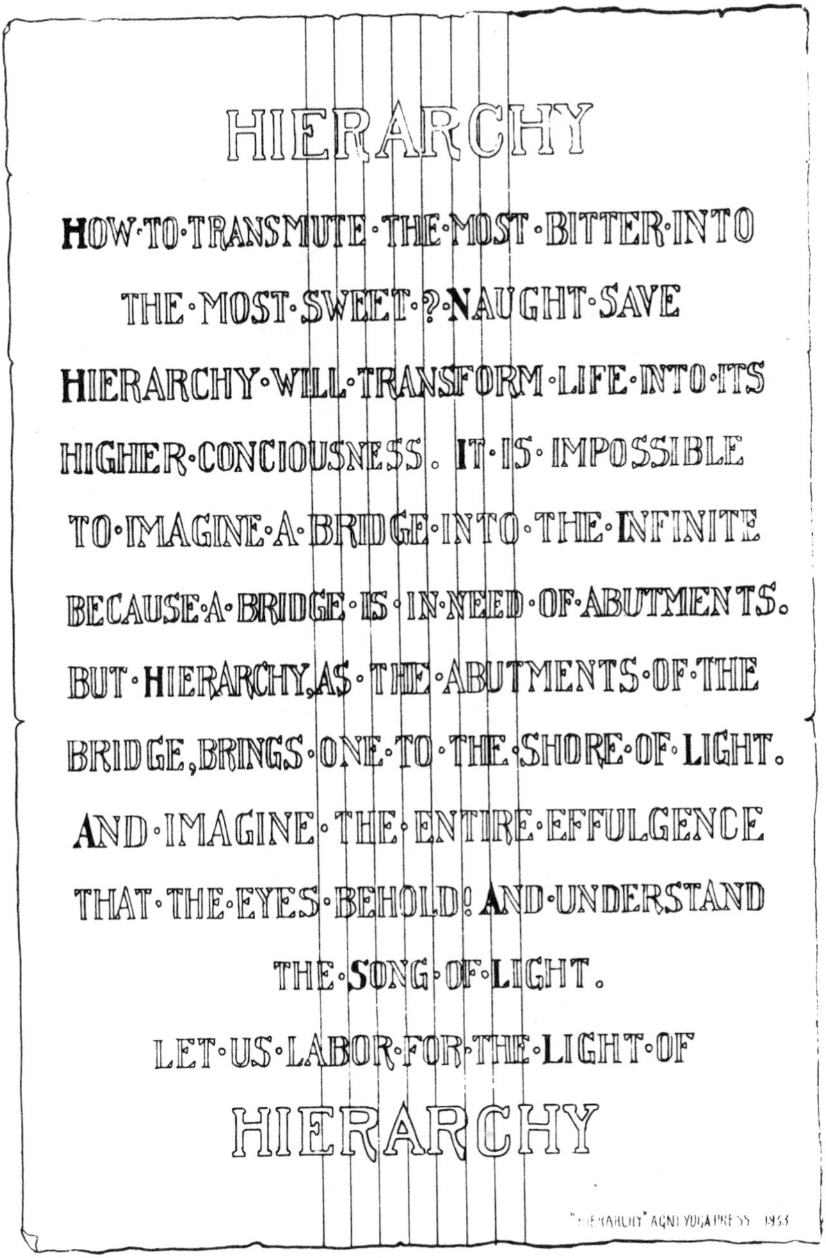

HIERARCHY

HOW·TO·TRANSMUTE·THE·MOST·BITTER·INTO
THE·MOST·SWEET·?·NAUGHT·SAVE
HIERARCHY·WILL·TRANSFORM·LIFE·INTO·ITS
HIGHER·CONCIOUSNESS。IT·IS·IMPOSSIBLE
TO·IMAGINE·A·BRIDGE·INTO·THE·INFINITE
BECAUSE·A·BRIDGE·IS·IN·NEED·OF·ABUTMENTS。
BUT·HIERARCHY,AS·THE·ABUTMENTS·OF·THE
BRIDGE,BRINGS·ONE·TO·THE·SHORE·OF·LIGHT。
AND·IMAGINE·THE·ENTIRE·EFFULGENCE
THAT·THE·EYES·BEHOLD!·AND·UNDERSTAND
THE·SONG·OF·LIGHT。
LET·US·LABOR·FOR·THE·LIGHT·OF

HIERARCHY

"HIERARCHY" AGNI YOGA PRESS 1933

DIAGRAM 9

successfully.

Since this may not be possible with many who read this book, we shall try to limit and direct its distribution in other ways. There are individuals for whom contact with our statements may stimulate ancient knowledge and bring them into the "danger zone" so often mentioned by true teachers. This could only come from unwise experiment and from directing attention to the true psychic centers or combining ideas with other techniques and pictures. What we give is amply protected if followed as given.

This beginning technique is designed to test the sincerity, persistence, aspiration, motivation, and initiative of the student. He or she must demonstrate that directions will be followed, because the results can only be achieved through personal and individual effort. The work done is fundamental and the result absolutely essential before any other type of work can be given.

The average applicant to this teaching has some radiance about the head and "the spark which hangs from the flame,"* although the tiny Soul Star above his head may be no more than a recognizable radiant point of light as seen by clairvoyant vision. He or she also has a noticeable degree of sensitivity and a recognized responsibility to serve mankind as much as possible. It has been found that this Soul Star will respond and become more active when the

---

*See Diagram 8 in the chapter "Reiteration," which shows the growth of this "spark" of Soul.

mind is centered upon it. When this occurs, the probationary test period of the individual work may be started. Although no one can predict the length of time any phase of this work will take, since it depends upon individual karma as well as upon the application, effort, and persistence of each individual who undertakes it, the average time is between two-to-three months. This is the effort made by the aspiring personality, but this effort alone is not enough. The Soul or inner spiritual self must cooperate; if the Soul cannot or will not cooperate, nothing can or will be done.

Invocation of the Soul

We have spoken earlier of the statement in the Bhagavad Gita in which the Soul says: "I put down a portion of myself but remain." This "portion" appears at first as an almost invisible spark, usually covered by an iridescent cluster of forms called "idealized thoughtforms." In aspirants, the spark is enlarged but still a small, pale globe of light. In those who have taken the first steps on the Path, it is bright and radiating somewhat. In initiates of the threshold, the light above the head, the spark of Soul Star, becomes much larger and more radiant; when activated, the brilliant radiance of the Soul Star may extend several feet. This star is the etheric symbol of that portion of the Soul "put down" into matter. It is linked with the Soul, first by a thread, and then by a band of expanding rainbow fire as fusion of personality and Soul proceeds. This thread, and later band, is the etheric-astral-mental portion of the Antahkarana or bridge which exists until final fusion of personality and Soul takes place. This Soul Star is the instrument or extension through which the Soul works and ultimately changes the physical body through a definite, scientific process, into a suitable vehicle through which It can function.

The personality may invoke and cooperate, but the Soul Star is an extension of the Soul and will not respond to personality demands or experiments except for those that further the Soul's own purpose. The Soul Star will not be expanded, exploded, whirled, projected or put through any personality gymnastics, and such efforts may interfere with its real function. Accordingly, the first approach of the personal self is to *invoke the Soul*.

Therefore, the prime necessity for any student learning how to "recognize, tap, channel and direct" spiritual energy is to enlist the cooperation of his own Soul in the project. One certain way to achieve this involves the use of a very ancient mantram. The mind should be centered or concentrated in the Soul Star, located at a point about six inches above the head, holding firmly in mind the idea of the Soul's cooperation with the aspiring personality. Then speak *aloud,* with a pause at the end of each line, the ancient mantram. Each of these statements of affirmation produce certain results in the subtle bodies which will become evident to students as time passes. The most significant result at this stage is the increase in the size, brilliance, and radiation of the Soul Star, indicating the eagerness of the Soul to cooperate with the personality and the Soul's willingness to begin the infusion with the higher types of energy and life. This mantram should become so much a part of the inner life that it is held constantly in the student's consciousness. *No work should be undertaken until this mantram has been said.* The words are as follows:

I am the Soul.
I am the Light Divine.
I am Love.
I am Will.
I am Fixed Design.

After the invocation or Soul Mantram has been said, the Soul Star will obey thought and move within the vehicles and the electromagnetic field. It will expand or contract or send out a beam of energy without personality direction. It will also differentiate its white radiance into energies, some of which have familiar colors. These are only beginning powers of the Soul Star. It is a most powerful, versatile, and useful instrument of White Magic. *It will not respond for anything else.*

Students generally understand the statements in the Soul Mantram, except for the last line. The "fixed design" refers to the plan of the Soul for the current incarnation. Within this plan, a man has freedom of choice and may live his life any way he wishes. If he makes mistakes, as all evolving men do, he will learn from them; however, if he follows the plan of the Soul, he will evolve more rapidly and reap the benefits of his incarnation.

This ancient Soul Mantram, given by the Tibetan Master, Dwal Khul, in the book Discipleship in the New Age, Volume II, page 123, is the first meditation outlined and it is the absolute beginning of *all* occult techniques. Without the use of this mantram, or some form of it, yoga practices, meditations, chantings, postures, breathings, and the like are ineffective in making changes in the inner vehicles. We have witnessed years of such practices which made *no change* in the inner vehicles of the aspirant. We have also witnessed that use of this mantram and its presence in the "brooding consciousness" of the student have made simple techniques rapidly effective in clearing and energizing the inner vehicles and in building radiant magnetic fields around purified forms. This is not to say that the dedicated and sincere work done by aspiring students has no effect whatever; it does test their dedication, persistence, and aspiration, and it is true that all "honest" effort produces a just reward.

With the use of the Soul Mantram, the aspirant activates the Soul Star which expands and intensifies its radiation. In the course of time, the remaining four lines have the following effects:

I AM THE LIGHT DIVINE.

The Central Channel flashes forth and intensifies. It becomes full of rainbow fire.

I AM LOVE.

A rose-pink downpour of energy from the heart of the Soul Star floods the Central Channel.

I AM WILL.

A royal purple, brilliant clear red, a white, or an indigo blue downpour enters and fills the Central Channel. Sometimes all of these energies are present or follow each other in sequence, and the order or sequence may vary.

I AM FIXED DESIGN.

The sensitive points along the Central Channel flash forth with intense radiation; these later are the points occupied by the psychic centers or chakras. Since the fixed design is the plan of the Soul for the current incarnation, it is indicated by the energy components in the vehicles and their relative strengths.

The above description of what occurs as the Soul Mantram is voiced are just the first noticeable reactions. Effects increase with time, application and progressive purification. As alignment with the Soul becomes stronger, and as personality integration develops, the ability of the lower bodies (mental, emotional and etheric-physical) to respond together *as a unit* becomes definite and other results are obtained.

In the Soul Mantram, the first line brings about identification with the Soul as a manifested entity on the mental plane, the Solar Angel. The second, third and fourth lines are spoken *as if* the aspirant were the Soul invoking its subjective being—atma, buddhi, manas, or spiritual will, spiritual love and higher mind. The fifth line states the plan or design of the Soul for the personality for this incarnation.

By using this "as if" technique, the personality begins to identify with the Soul. After the personality begins to cooperate with and acquiesce to the Soul, it begins the work of building the Body of Light.* The Body of Light is built by the Soul as a substitute for the absorbed personality.

The Soul Does the Work

In relation to human personalities, the Soul is the true incarnator. It knows nothing of the lower planes except that which it contacts and retrieves through the lower bodies. Its manifestation on the lower levels is limited to that portion of Itself which we call the Soul Star through which we receive a minute part of Soul-consciousness called Self-Consciousness.

After eons of time, the personal Soul vested in the Soul Star awakens and turns its attention toward its source, its Father in Heaven, with aspiration; it begins to cooperate in Soul intent, and the Soul's response is instantaneous and joyous. The Soul's meditative attention becomes concentrated and rapid progress in Soul-personality integration can be consummated.

---

*The Body of Light is also referred to as the Mayavirupa in Esoteric Healing, by Alice A. Bailey, page 518.

The ancient teaching impresses us with the need for the personal self *to act as if* it is the Soul *as far as possible,* and to realize that the Soul's objectives are not those of the personal self and that the Soul's wisdom and power are far beyond the comprehension of the personal self. Therefore, the personal self uses the Soul Mantram, "I am the Soul . . . ." We repeat—this mantram should become a central part of your consciousness and realization. Without this affirmation no technique of mind, emotional nature or physical action has any subjective result; such practices only stir the physical body, demonstrate persistence and strengthen aspiration. *The outer forms of the techniques we give are without result if not preceded by this Soul Mantram.*

It is the Soul that does the work, that builds the Central Channel, sensitizes the points along the Channel to later receive the psychic centers, uses the Spiritual Whirlwind (described later), releases invoked energies to the aspiring student, raises the energies of substance and matter to blend with the invoked energies, builds the Body of Light, and ultimately absorbs the personal self.

Cooperation of the personal self in the form of persistence, fiery aspiration, and focused attention while following the techniques, is needed and required for success. It is as if the Soul said, "I am here; be still and know that I will do all that is needed." Building the Central Channel is a cooperative effort between the Soul and the personal self, even if not a great deal is required of the personality.

The Central Vertical Channel

We have spoken of the "thread" which is the beginning of the bridge. There are successive additions to this central thread until five main strands are complete.* As a bridge in consciousness on the mental plane, the Antahkarana or Rainbow Bridge is described as a symbolic triangle. The first link is made between the personality, as an energy center called the Mental Unit, and between the Soul, focused in the Causal Body or Egoic Lotus. It is this relationship which is vitalized by the affirmation, "I am the Soul . . . ." The successive statements relate to the Spiritual Triad focused on the highest mental level, and the final statement relates to the link between the abstract mind and the personal self focused in the concrete mind — the Mental Unit. Changes in the Central Vertical Channel show the completion of these linkages and the growth in spiritual attainment.

Many of the pictures, plates and sketches in this book show the vertical line or lines connecting various planes, aspects, or vehicles. All of these are aspects of the bridge or Antahkarana. Technically, it is described as a five-fold thread. The life thread is the beginning which links the highest energies of the planet to the lowest.

Two threads are projected by the Soul; three

---

* These additions are described by Dwal Khul in <u>Education in the New Age</u>, page 143, and in <u>The Rays and the Initiations</u> in the chapter called "The Science of the Antahkarana," pages 441-501. There are also references to the "channel" in <u>Letters on Occult Meditation</u>.

threads are projected by the personality, making a five-fold thread. When the two and the three are linked to the throat center, man becomes a conscious creator.

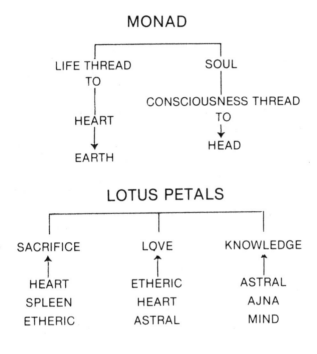

MONAD

LIFE THREAD	SOUL
TO	
↓	CONSCIOUSNESS THREAD
HEART	TO
↓	↓
EARTH	HEAD

LOTUS PETALS

SACRIFICE	LOVE	KNOWLEDGE
↑	↑	↑
HEART	ETHERIC	ASTRAL
SPLEEN	HEART	AJNA
ETHERIC	ASTRAL	MIND

THE FIVE STRANDS
OF THE ANTAHKARANA

The Science of the Antahkarana deals, therefore, with the entire incoming system of energy, with the processes of usage and transformation and fusion. It deals also with the outgoing energies and their relationship to the environment and is the basis of the science of the force centers.

That the Antahkarana is described as both a
triangle of energy, or that it is described as a
bridge in consciousness on the mental plane,
should not confuse the student. The reason for
these variations in description is that space and
time are not the same on other levels as they are
on the physical plane, and the effort to find
correct analogies and descriptive words sometimes appears paradoxical or misleading. Objectively, to clairvoyant vision, the Antahkarana is
manifested in the Central Vertical Channel and
its condition and use and development is revealed
there.

Although the activation and expansion of the
Central Channel is necessary for the individual
clearing processes, its most important aspect is
its linking between the Planetary Logos and His
physical vehicle, Earth, as well as its importance
as a transmitter of His energies through ourselves
as units of intelligence within His body.

The most important construction job anyone
will ever undertake is to build this Central
Channel through which spiritual energies can
flow and begin their redemptive work. This
channel has been called by various names by
different teachers and systems—the rod or staff,
the middle pillar, the axis, the rainbow bridge,
the Antahkarana. Ultimately, this channel forms
the link between highest spirit and lowest matter.

Techniques

The technique used to build the Central
Channel is called *triangulation* because it consists

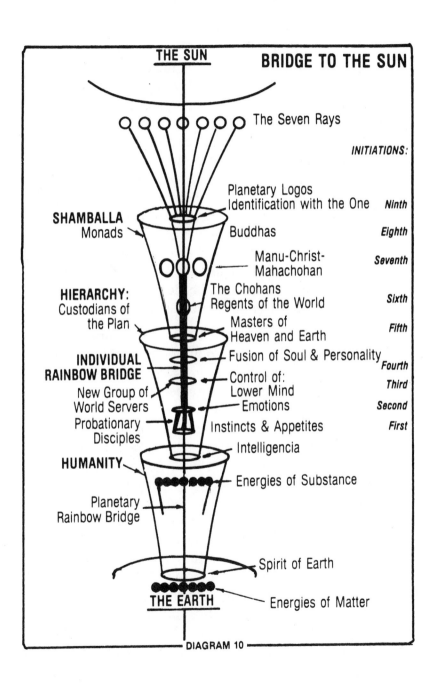

THE SUN

BRIDGE TO THE SUN

The Seven Rays

INITIATIONS:

SHAMBALLA
Monads

Planetary Logos
Identification with the One — Ninth

Buddhas — Eighth

Manu-Christ-
Mahachohan — Seventh

HIERARCHY:
Custodians of
the Plan

The Chohans
Regents of the World — Sixth

Masters of
Heaven and Earth — Fifth

INDIVIDUAL
RAINBOW BRIDGE

Fusion of Soul & Personality — Fourth

New Group of
World Servers

Control of:
Lower Mind — Third

Emotions — Second

Probationary
Disciples

Instincts & Appetites — First

Intelligencia

HUMANITY

Energies of Substance

Planetary
Rainbow Bridge

Spirit of Earth

THE EARTH

Energies of Matter

DIAGRAM 10

of building, mentally and imaginatively, a series
of small triangles, one side of which, when
aligned, forms the vertical channel. It is an occult
truism to say that _energy follows thought._ This
is a literal and very important fact. As we direct
our thought to the Soul Star, and invoke its
response through the mind and mental processes
of imagination and visualization, it is possible
for us to direct the movement of the star with its
Soul energy in a controlled manner. By this
mental direction of energy, a student is able to
clear away a channel for the continuous flow of
spiritual energies which pass through the lower
vehicles or bodies. This is a slow and gradual
process because it must be done under control
and without haste or carelessness.

It should be mentioned that the points along
the Central Channel used in the formation of the
triangles are _not_ the major psychic centers; they
are substitutes for the major centers at this stage.
The substitute centers or sensitive points along
the Central Channel are constructed by the
creative imagination. It is perhaps unfortunate at
this stage that they have been given names and
locations with reference to the physical vehicle;
however, if it is _clearly understood_ that the
substitute centers are the product of the creative
imagination, no harm will be done and the names
and locations will have future value. The real
energy centers are outside the body due to the
"loaded" condition of the vehicles. Later, when
the channel becomes clear and straight, full of
spiritual light and quite large, and the external
thoughtforms have been removed, the major

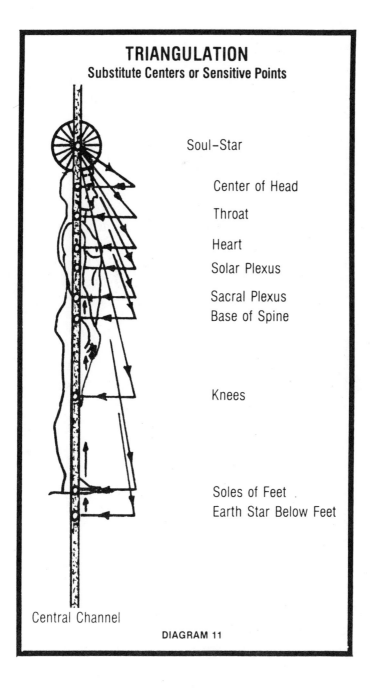

TRIANGULATION
Substitute Centers or Sensitive Points

Soul-Star

Center of Head

Throat

Heart
Solar Plexus

Sacral Plexus
Base of Spine

Knees

Soles of Feet
Earth Star Below Feet

Central Channel

DIAGRAM 11

centers will move into position at intervals where they belong along the channel.

It is suggested that, in the beginning, only the first triangle (involving the center between the eyes) be formed during the practice session for at least two weeks. In the third week two more points—the throat and heart—may be added. The fourth week add the solar plexus; the fifth week add the sacral plexus; the sixth week add the base of the spine. Each week thereafter, add one or two of the remaining points (at the knees, the soles of the feet, and the Earth Star, six inches below the feet) until all triangles have been made and the Central Channel is completely through the body and anchored to the earth.

Always move the Soul Star very slowly and deliberately in its upward motion. As in any container, the heavier material in the body sinks to the bottom and requires more effort to remove it. When starting on the minor points or substitute centers, do the upper points more quickly and spend more time on the lower ones in order to bring the Central Channel into even and equal development all the way through. There must be no blockage or tapering off of the channel; if there is, there may be a dispersion of energy at that point and consequently unpleasant and unfavorable effects. It is better to practice this technique too long and too much than to neglect any part of it.

The exact technique used to build the Central Channel is as follows:

STEP ONE: Repeat the Soul Mantram, aloud if possible.

STEP TWO: Concentrate your attention in the Soul Star six inches above your head. If you cannot see it or sense it, visualize or imagine it as a small, brilliant sun. You will recognize its presence in time.

STEP THREE: Mentally move the Soul Star diagonally forward to a position just in front of the eyes, straight into the center of the head, and *slowly* move the Soul Star straight upward to the position six inches above the head. Repeat this triangulation two or three more times.

This procedure should be followed for each sensitive point marked in the sequence given in Diagram 11. Since the Central Channel is made of etheric matter, it is not affected by the position of the body, that is, sitting or standing, or lying down.

Those who have some knowledge in the kaleidoscopic field of occult investigation may take note and question what is obvious in our diagrams and descriptions, namely, that the Central Channel, the bridge, continues beyond vision *into the earth* as well as upward (the traditional direction of Heaven). This linkage to Earth was not emphasized by Dwal Khul, probably for the reason that in the past, efforts of many magicians (both developed and amateur) have focused on the Earth energies—energies of matter: earth, water, air and fire. These Earth energies are the precipitating energies of materialization, and in their connection with the devic or angelic forces (the builders of form), they must be used for that last and most difficult step in evolution or descent into form. The higher correspondences of these energies were generally omitted by magicians which resulted in an unbalanced condition and led to cases of unspeakable perversions and ceremonies ranging from the ridiculous to the most vicious and destructive. Such usage creates very bad karma for these practitioners.

Dwal Khul has said, ". . . the Hierarchy need not be further handicapped by working in substance while the forces of evil work both in substance and matter."[1] This prophecy has been implemented by the recognition that man is a child of Earth as well as of Heaven. Hierarchy also is working in matter now. Consequently, Earth as the body of the Planetary Logos will be purified as the process of externalization continues.

The Spiritual Whirlwind or Etheric Vortex

The clouded condition of the electromagnetic field or aura around the vehicles—mental, emotional or astral, and etheric-physical—of all persons, without exception, as seen by clairvoyant vision, and described further in this book under "Purification of the Vehicles," is quite undesirable. The Tibetan Master has spoken of this condition as "fogs and miasmas," and its accu-

---

[1]Externalization of the Hierarchy, by Alice A. Bailey, page 689.

mulation is from two main sources: contact with the fields of others, both individual, collective and planetary; and the product of the destruction of more resistant thoughtforms in building, burning through, for the Central Channel and later from the disintegration of the more resistant thoughtforms that adhere to the bodies.

In the process of building the Central Channel, the Antahkarana, the Soul Star literally burns its way through hindering thoughtforms and complexes to open a channel for the flow of higher energies. This produces debris which must be cleared from the vehicles and fields.

This debris is a constant burden and menace to all and must be disposed of continually. There comes a time when the Causal Field or Soul Body becomes organized and intense enough to burn most of this gathered debris on contact. Until that time, an instrument of the Soul, called the Spiritual Whirlwind or Etheric Vortex, can be used to sweep this debris out of the field.

This Etheric Vortex is built of energy-substance of the highest etheric subplanes of the etheric-physical, emotional and lower mental planes and is generally white in color, indicative of the seventh (highest) atomic subplane. The vortex is a spiritual reality which is invoked *as if* we were the Soul with the creative imagination "deliberately stimulated, mentally appreciated and emotionally propelled." The vortex removes the substance loosened and remaining in the field after the triangulation process for the day is completed. Dwal Khul has said much about this vortex, which He calls "the funnel." Its elementary use is to clear away the loose debris in the field, but it has a great many more uses also.[*]

To explain the vortex and how it works, it is necessary to use an analogy. It has been found in nature that air or water moving downward under the law of gravity forms a vortex, whirlpool, or cyclone. Three forces enter into the formation of a tornado: gravity, centifugal force (outward-dispersion) and centripetal (inward-attractive) force. With these three in approximate balance, the form is maintained. A vacuum forms at the empty center and heavier objects are carried into the vortex by currents of air moving to fill the vacuum at the center and are rotated in the rim, thrown off, or drawn down into the center.

Analogous principles and applications can be used to explain the vortex which is a rotating whirl of etheric energy. The vortex is started by focusing the mind in visualization far above the head outside the Causal Field (Soul Body). This causes a downward rush of higher and more rarified energy-substance into lower and denser energy-substance. This energy is invoked by personality unification with the Soul, by visualization of the vortex by the student and projection by the Soul. The tip or lowest point of the vortex follows the Central Channel (or the fine

---

[*] "By means of this 'funnel' which penetrates from the physical to the emotional, or still higher to one or the other of the mental levels, the Intelligences or Powers are enabled to pour forth illuminating light or power or some kind or other into those who thus approach Them. The 'funnel' forms a 'channel' whereby the contact can be made." - Letters on Occult Meditation, by Alice A. Bailey, page 191-2

thread, like a strand of spider web, which exists in everyone). As it moves downward, picking up the heavier substance not locked into the vehicles in thoughtforms, it sweeps away any loose and drifting substance which adheres to the field as the result of daily contacts with people and the environment. When the disciple is in contact with many people, he should use this vortexing technique to clear the etheric refuse in the fields of those around him. While this benefits the disciple, it also benefits those in proximity to him whose fields are cleared by the energies of the vortex of the dross and debris which they normally carry. The vortex picks up the unwanted debris in the field and carries it deep into the Earth where it is used to benefit the lower kingdoms evolving with humanity on the planet. All forms are constantly processing energy-substance; receiving, assimilating, eliminating. The spiritual vortex accelerates part of this system in a kind of spiritual ecology.

Until the disciple can sense when to cease invocation of the vortex, he should use it for at least five minutes after the Phase I work has been done. This assures the removal of debris which has been loosened in the process of clearing the central channel. The size of the vortex and the frequencies (colors) used, as well as the direction, are determined by the Soul which sometimes takes over from the visualized program with a program of Its own. This need not be of concern to students if, indeed, such control is recognized. As the vortex gains strength and power, it follows the cycle of clearing without constant

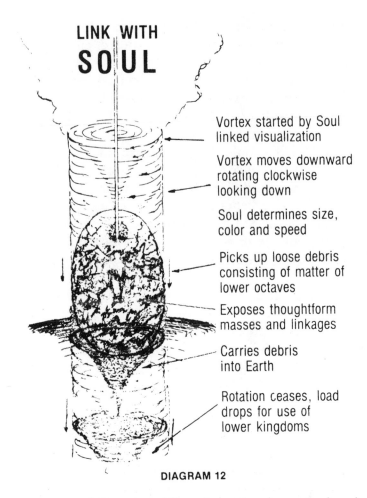

LINK WITH SOUL

Vortex started by Soul linked visualization

Vortex moves downward rotating clockwise looking down

Soul determines size, color and speed

Picks up loose debris consisting of matter of lower octaves

Exposes thoughtform masses and linkages

Carries debris into Earth

Rotation ceases, load drops for use of lower kingdoms

DIAGRAM 12

personal direction. Therefore, the size, speed and nature of the energy used are all controlled by the Soul and do not require personal direction and guidance.

The vortex must not be interfered with by overzealous aspirants, but must be allowed to pass completely through and outside the Causal Field where, with its load of debris, it disappears in a zone or layer of the etheric body of the planet, which we call the etheric fire or "burning ground." (The term "burning ground" also has more subjective occult applications.) The Whirlwind *does not* then hover around, move forward, and up again to the point where it entered the field upon invocation. When it drops its load which it carries out of the field and into the Earth, it simply ceases to move and disappears. A "new" vortex of energy must be invoked; it is possible to invoke a whole series of Whirlwinds to move through the vehicles and fields, giving the appearance of a column of light or Soul Fire, moving through to the "burning ground," twenty to thirty feet below the earth. *The Whirlwind is not a thing,* although it has been called a "tool of the Soul."

As we have said, when attention is turned away from the vortex and its movement deep within the Earth, it stops rotating, drops its load and ceases to exist. Diagram 12 shows the steps in this process which, when carried on consistently, clears the vehicles and their radiating magnetic fields of loose and contaminating debris, and internal smog, which is constantly drawn toward and into the vehicles until radiating powers are attained to offset the effects of the heavy fields and inner smogs of humanity.

It should be noted that this process of clearing with the Whirlwind, at this stage of the work, should be continued from three to five minutes. It is always better to use this practical and useful tool, the vortex, longer than is required. It should be used not only during and after the daily work (upon completion of the technique of Phase I) but frequently during the day.

The question will occur to students: how can the aspirant know when the process is needed and when is it complete? To recognize this is a part of the training in sensitivity, the beginning of etheric, emotional and mental sense perception. Some aspirants "see" and "feel" or "sense" immediately. All arrive at a point very soon when the condition of the field shows to inner vision that they have somehow sensed when they are not clear.

The process of clearing the vehicles and field of loose debris, silt, and objectionable substance with the vortex works rapidly, but still takes measurable time, and the process must be repeated until such debris is gone. This is an *elimination process* which is a basic part of the clearing technique, and it must be used constantly throughout the purification of the vehicles. The Whirlwind will not dislodge the denser thoughtforms or cage; another technique must be used in connection with the Whirlwind and the next technique, Phase II, describes the beginning of it.

Widening the Central Channel

In the first phase of building the Central Channel, the disciple has linked himself with Hierarchy and become a bridge for those energies which will enable the Logos to implement His Plan of raising the vibration of the planet.

After a time, the Central Channel begins to expand; strand after strand of living, vibrant energy clothed in color are added and, at a certain apparent size, there appears to clairvoyant vision a steady flow of rainbow fire from beyond vision, through the individual, into the Earth. Within the bodies of the disciple-initiate, the Central Channel (the enlarged thread) increases in diameter and intensity of light and the whole body is irradiated.

The second phase of work is more personal. It is aimed at eliminating those ancient thought-forms which stand between the disciple and the truth and prevent his fusion with the Soul.

However, before the purification work can be done effectively, the Central Channel must be widened to a diameter of at least one inch. A cleanly developed one-inch diameter channel is sufficient to carry the energy needed for second phase work of clearing external thoughtform clusters. However, continued work expands the channel to four or five inches. As the high pressure subjective energies pass through the channel, radiation occurs. Such radiation is strongly purifying as long as the simple techniques of its activation are continued. Once a certain growth and condition of the Central Channel is attained, processes can be used to speed this purification. Since the Soul responds immediately to the efforts of the personal self to link with its Higher Self, changes in the etheric substance of the vehicles proceed rapidly. These processes outlined are the next phase of the work, Phase II, and are given under the heading "Purification of the Vehicles."

The method used to widen the channel is outlined as follows:

STEP ONE: Say the Soul Mantram, and identify your consciousness with the Soul.

STEP TWO: Then say the Mantram of Unification:

> "The sons of men are one
> and I am one with them.
> I seek to love, not hate;
> I seek to serve and not exact due service;
> I seek to heal, not hurt.
>
> Let pain bring due reward of light and love.
> Let the Soul control the outer form
> and life and all events,
> And bring to light the love which underlies
> the happenings of the time.
>
> Let vision come and insight.
> Let the future stand revealed.
> Let inner union demonstrate and
> outer cleavages be gone.
> Let love prevail.
> Let all men love."

STEP THREE: Proceed with one large triangle to the place of the Earth Star beneath your feet. You do not need to make all the smaller triangles first; the one large triangle is sufficient.

STEP FOUR: As you move the Soul Star up the channel, visualize it moving in a clockwise corkscrew motion boring a path through the channel up to the position six inches above the head. The intention is to widen the channel as much as possible; IT MUST BE AT LEAST ONE INCH IN DIAMETER FOR SECOND PHASE WORK TO BE DONE EFFECTIVELY.

STEP FIVE: Vortex completely, with the usual clockwise vortex.

STEP SIX: End this process by saying the Great Invocation:

"From the point of Light within the Mind of God
Let Light stream forth into the minds of men.
Let Light descend on Earth.

From the point of Love within the Heart of God
Let Love stream forth into the hearts of men.
May Christ return to Earth.

From the center where the Will of God is known
Let purpose guide the little wills of men—
    The purpose which the Masters know and
    serve.

From the center which we call the race of men
Let the Plan of Love and Light work out.
    And may it seal the door where evil dwells.

Let Light and Love and Power restore the Plan on
Earth."

Repeat this process twice a day for approximately two weeks.

After the Central Channel has been widened to at least one inch in diameter, it is of a sufficient size to carry the energies required to break up and disintegrate those ancient obstructions which color one's perceptions of and reactions to one's environment.

CHAPTER VI

PHASE II—
PURIFICATION OF THE VEHICLES

". . . Thou shalt separate the earth from the
fire and subtle from the gross,
gently with much sagacity . . . "
—Emerald Tablet of Hermes

Through patient and persistent effort with use
of the techniques of Phase I, a Central Channel
one inch in diameter has been built from the Soul
Star through the mental, emotional, and vital or
etheric bodies. This clear, radiant, energy path is
now used to begin the long process of clearing or,
in the old terminology, purification of the vehicles
and their radiating field, the aura.

Every religious movement and spiritual teacher
has emphasized the need for purification, but the
purification required has nearly always been inter-
preted in physical terms—to practice celibacy, to

be a vegetarian, to fast and pray, to keep the body clean, to observe certain dietary practices, etc. These have all been essential guidelines for humanity during the time when men were victims of their uncontrolled appetites and instincts. However, purification means a great deal more than this; it means purifying the lower instruments of all hindrances to fusion with the Soul and a transforming of the very substance of these instruments so that Soul infusion will be possible. This deeper and more fundamental purification can only be done through the scientific use of energy.

Energy is not a vague, amorphous "something" which we can classify as "spiritual" and then confidently expect it to do the purification work with no effort on our part. The scientific use of energy enables the disciple to devote his efforts to a process of clearing, to understand what the process is, why it is used, and what it accomplishes as sequential steps are taken. The second phase of our work emphasizes the disciple's ability to "tap, channel and direct" energies.

EVOLUTION OF TECHNIQUES

"When a man can see a need for correction and for adjustment in a brother's vehicle, and can awaken in his brother a desire to adjust that which is amiss, wise assistance can be given by the one who sees and sounds."
—A Treatise on Cosmic Fire, page 452

In our long lives we have experimented with many techniques, many types of meditation, many different groups, and between us we have touched, at least lightly, almost all of those conventional and generally accepted and publicized methods of approach to the teachings of the Ancient Wisdom.

In the course of our experience, we came in contact with a disciple experimenting with a way to clear the vehicles of those obstructions referred to in numerous ways as complexes, or engrams, or thoughtforms,* and which Dwal Khul calls "obstacles, hindrances and distractions."

We had been able to observe, through clairvoyant vision, that these obstructions and thoughtforms did exist; however, the fact was that it had not occurred to us that they could be eliminated. The universality of the clouded fields of all of the disciples we had contacted led us to accept this condition as being the natural condition of the vehicles and not subject to immediate change. It was generally thought that the "fogs and miasmas" and general obstructions which Dwal Khul spoke of were to be cleared sometime in the far distant future.

---

*These clusters are hindrances, obstacles and distractions which stand between a disciple and the truth. These were recognized by the early Kahunas as mentioned in Max Freedom Long's The Secret Science Behind Miracles, as well as in many places in Dwal Khul's writings. See also the picture in this book and comments regarding Mme. Blavatsky's precipitation of the aura of Mr. Stainton Moseyn.

While the disciple we encountered had some astral and etheric clairvoyance, enabling him to see the Soul Star when it had any development, we were not accustomed to his methods of using word-form combinations with overtones of the mentalist approach of affirmation and denial. His methods had a definite material, objective focus instead of the usual aspirational, invocative meditative form. Nevertheless, we supported his efforts, mostly as an experiment to see what could be done along the lines which he suggested. Our attitude in this experiment was to assist—to stay in the background and put him forward as the leader of the groups which were formed.

We formed groups for him and supported him for many years in the hope that changes could be made. However, in the end, our vision did not confirm what he asserted to be facts and conditions. Although our observations did not agree with his, we did notice some changes in the fields—a stirring and partial clearing of the fogs and miasmas and a stirring of the clusters of dark shapes in the aura which were more concentrated and denser as they got closer to the body. These shapes and forms appeared to be an extension of the denser masses near the body. Although in a few cases these forms appeared to "shrink" somewhat with the techniques he used, they *were not eliminated.*

In spite of growing difficulties, we persisted with this work, because it seemed to us that these thoughtform clusters could be eliminated, due to the fact that we experienced a shrinkage of some of them when we did the work. The effects *on us* were not the same as in others and we could not understand that. When we got deeper into the work there were manifestations and etheric materializations which only we could see.

We summed up our experience with the conclusion that although the fields of the students were stirred by the techniques used, the results were not consistent enough to warrant presentation of these techniques to the public or to any group of disciples with any certainty of success. Yet, it seemed to us that there were possibilities in this approach, even though something was missing.

Upon leaving this group, we were asked to teach a small group of students interested in Dwal Khul's works. When we were alone with this new group, it became rapidly apparent why the techniques of the previous group had been only slightly effective. We found that the missing element was the *Invocation of the Soul.* As soon as we invoked the Soul, we got definite results in the "purification" of the fields.

In these first experiments we worked intensely on our own vehicles, keeping records and taking voluminous notes of the effects and results. The processes of purification of the vehicles proceeded gradually. By the time we were well into the work of purification, we discovered that there were gradual changes taking place in the electromagnetic field, in the atomic structure of the body, and along the threads or nadis which compose the etheric body.

The sequence of observed events included:

1. The enlargement of the Central Buddhic thread into what we call the Central Vertical Channel;

2. The clearing of "debris" which corresponds to what Dwal Khul calls "fogs and miasmas;"

3. The elimination of the "cage;"

4. Gradual, yet steady, elimination of those thoughtforms observed in the vehicles.

It was by applying the three Laws of Purification, Redemption and Applied Energy mentioned by Dwal Khul to a deeper extent that we succeeded in clearing the external accumulation of thoughtforms retained in clusters outside of the physical vehicles. The work was successful, with all, depending upon the persistence and mental capacity of the individual student. Only the time required varied.

Eventually, we brought all in the group to a point where they could undertake more advanced work. We did not require long and extremely disciplined meditative practices, or breathing exercises, or chantings, or any of the other standard methods of the past; and yet, all in the group who did the clearing work came to the point where they recognized their intuitive nature, increased their capacities, and made great progress. The fact that the Soul was invoked and responded moved everyone ahead very rapidly, and led us to the basic underlying conclusion *the Soul does the work.*

Later, with some experimental changes in the techniques used, we discovered how to eliminate the obstructions in the interior of the etheric vehicle. With ourselves, for we always experimented on ourselves first, we cleared such barriers to a point where we speeded up the changes in the atomic and etheric structure of our vehicles. This Dwal Khul describes as among the changes necessary in the initiatory process.

In our focus upon techniques, we do not mean to suggest that Dwal Khul did not give any. In fact, His books are full of suggestions indicating how the subject of techniques should be approached. In connection with His group of disciples, described in Discipleship in the New Age, Volumes I and II, there were many techniques suggested. Unfortunately, individuals were allowed to pass upon their personal instructions as to what was published and, in most cases, deleted instructions as to techniques.

There is a comprehensive thought back of all techniques, that is, as we have said, our vehicles of manifestation must be changed. This change is in the way of refinement of existing structures, rather than additions. It should be remembered that the Path is a movement in consciousness "upward" from involvement in dense forms to those of greater freedom and beauty. We must add here that it is not only a movement in consciousness that is required, but a *change in the very substance of the vehicles on all personality levels.* Without such change the vehicles cannot register or evaluate the higher energies involved in advanced teaching. This accounts for the rather cryptic commentary so often made in Dwal Khul's writings that certain statements cannot be understood until certain advancements are made which are measured and acknowledged by the initiations.

To those aspirants who believe that intellectual training and analytical capacities of the concrete mind can do everything, we refer to what Dwal Khul has said, that

> ...the mysteries are revealed, not primarily by the reception of information anent them and their processes, but by the action of certain processes, carried out within the etheric body of the disciple. These enable him to know that which is hidden...[1]

Since our emphasis is on techniques, and the way to make those changes necessary in the vehicles, we repeat what has already been mentioned, that the liberation of the Soul comes about through the salvation of matter, or as Dwal Khul has said:

> ...that the liberation of the Soul or Ego comes about when Its work of salvaging matter (through utilizing it and building it into forms) has been carried forward to a desired point. It is not primarily due to the attainment of a certain spiritual stature by the man and the demonstration of certain spiritual qualities. This desired stature and these spiritual qualities are manifested when the vehicles have been 'occultly

---

[1] The Rays and the Initiations, by Alice A. Bailey, p. 337

saved,' and the matter has thus been transformed, transmuted, and symbolically 'raised
up into heaven.' When the vehicles vibrate in
unison with the Soul, then is liberation
achieved.[2]

Our work and the techniques used are aimed at
achieving this liberation of the Soul through the
salvaging of the matter of the lower vehicles.
However, this is a program which the disciple
undertakes which Dwal Khul has called a "forcing process." Again, quoting from Externalization of the Hierarchy, page 17:

> These men and women have ... subjected them-
> selves to a *forcing process* which is intended to
> bring the full power of the Soul into *premature
> blossoming*, and this in order more rapidly and
> effectively to serve the race, and to cooperate
> with the plan of the Hierarchy.*

We could paraphrase these three quotations by
saying that: first, the mysteries are revealed and
initiate powers are gained by *changes in the
vehicles* and not by the accumulation of information "anent" the mysteries; second, the liberation
of the Soul comes about when the matter of the
vehicles is *salvaged*, and not by the attaining of
spiritual status, as usually understood; and third,
what must be done to accomplish those changes
is brought about by a *forcing process* or *enforced
evolution.*

---

[2] A Treatise on the Seven Rays, Volume II, by Alice A.
Bailey, page 51, emphasis added.

*Emphasis added.

As we have emphasized, one of the strong injunctions given by Dwal Khul was that students must modify, qualify and adapt His teachings to suit time, place and circumstance, indicating that what He had given was to be the foundation, outline and basis for such modifications. Our work and the techniques used by our group have followed this injunction.

We can only restate that the techniques given, when faithfully followed, are *successful* in clearing the field of the accumulations of ancient and outworn thoughtforms and image complexes, which stand between the disciple and the truth. Elimination of these outworn thoughtforms helps to raise the vibration of the personality vehicles, thus making the student a more powerful and effective worker for Humanity and Hierarchy.

THE APPEARANCE OF THE FIELD

Most people, inwardly, look like walking thunder clouds—dark and turbulent and dangerous and quite unpleasant, except for the few who show radiance in the upper area of the electromagnetic field (aura) and the bright point of light overhead. (See Diagram 13.) Most people are almost entirely obscured by the heavy load they carry around. Sensitive people feel this heavy atmosphere of others around them and generally tend to shun crowds and all but a certain few whom they find tolerable. Of course, others feel the same way about them. This cloudy, unplea-

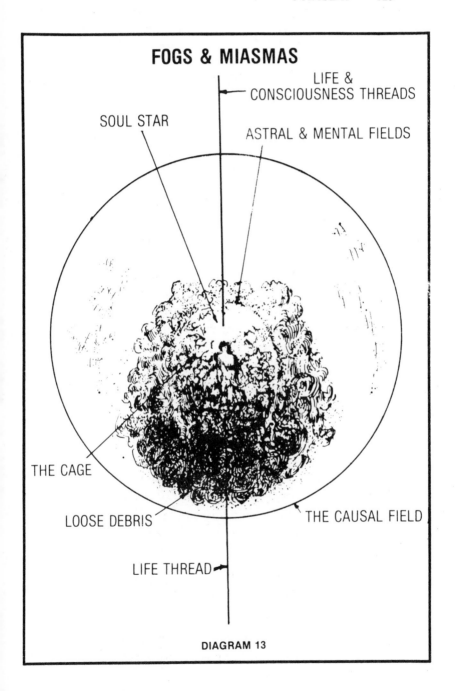

FOGS & MIASMAS

DIAGRAM 13

sant "mess" is the effluvia from their own bodies
—dead and discarded material they have not completely eliminated—it is also a collection they have
magnetized to themselves and allowed to gather in
the aura as they move through the activities of
daily life. This constitutes the "cloud," the loose,
churning material that fills the energy structures
known as the subtle bodies—etheric or vital,
astral or emotional, and the lower mental body or
the concrete mind.

In addition to the loose material around a
person, there is a more permanent and denser
structure which may be termed the "cage" because
it encloses and shuts the individual off entirely
from the outside world, and distorts every stream
of energy either sent to or from him. Without the
"cloud" of loose material, this cage appears as a
loosely organized series of linked distortions
which move with the disciple through every act of
his life. (See Diagram 14.) These distortions
appear to extrude from within, although the seeds
for their growth incarnate with the man; his reactions to his life and experiences cause them to
grow and to take form. They are representative of
habitual reactions to the events of living. Each
person has built the cage and the thoughtforms of
which it is composed *himself* and the "seeds" for
the cage and thoughtforms on all levels are carried
from life-to-life awaiting the time when the
personal self turns with invocation to the Soul for
their elimination.

Close to the body and adhering to it are
heavier, more resistant agglomerations of energy-

THE CAGE

Denser material
adhering to body

Soul Star obscured by
idealized thought forms

Fields cleared of debris,
revealing cage of retained
thought forms

DIAGRAM 14

substance which are extremely individual, and of
an even more limiting nature. These have been
seen by clairvoyants who have thought, quite
reasonably, that they were a mark of individuality; they are—but they are undesirable
residue from the past and must be removed
through the processes of purification or clearing.

DESCRIPTION OF THOUGHTFORMS

During the long period of growth and evolution, each human being has accumulated
thoughtforms which restrict the free expression of
the spiritual Self. Evolution of consciousness has
been an extremely slow and arduous process,
largely achieved by trial and error and by discarding old ideas and notions as new and better
ones have been found. However, much of the
"discarded old" still clings to the field in one
form or another and must be *eliminated from the
vehicles*. Roughly, these discards fall into five
types which are located in five different zones of
the body:

1. Those above the head and down as far as the
neck which are in the nature of false or outgrown
ideas or ideals. These are called the "idealized"
thoughtforms and relate to the mind. Many of
these idealized thoughtforms consist of true ideas
precipitated on the lower mental planes as ideals
suited to the development and environment of the
creator. Customs, codes, conventions, rules of
conduct, commandments, idols, angels and Gods,
high motivations of all kinds find their repre-
sentation here and remain even when outgrown
and replaced by later development. They stand
between the personal self and the true ideas
needed for further spiritual growth and must
eventually be eliminated.

2. Those about the neck and upper back,
shoulders and chest which seem to pertain largely
to negative ideas and feelings about personal

value or worth (although there are also some positive patterns of self-evaluation); these are called the "worthless" patterns of self-evaluation complexes, and their accumulation involve the emotional nature.

3. Those around the mid-section of the body are composed of more destructive feelings like hate, fear, anger and extremes of selfishness. Also in this region of the body are patterns of helpfulness (which is often interference), possessive love, and patterns produced by attitudes of sacrifice which make a person into a self-created martyr; these are all the result of misdirected emotion. These are called the "emotional images."

4. Those gathered in the lower torso area and about the hips and lower back are related to the instincts which are all rooted in fear—self-preservation, herding, sex, animal curiosity, self-assertion, the sense of possession, the belief that one is separate. These are the instinctual images of the etheric-physical vehicles.

5. The patterns clustered around the feet represent conditions in life that a person would like to run away from but cannot; they inhibit action and motion and are powerfully restrictive on the physical plane.

As we move downward through the five zones already described in our consideration of these accumulations, we find thoughtforms of increasing density relating to the emotional nature, the instinctual nature and to the physical body itself, in which case accumulations around the legs and feet actually inhibit movement in ways which affect the body itself as the body ages.

There are many people in the world today who have some clairvoyant faculty but very few who have mastered the many levels of consciousness full development requires. There is much conflicting opinion among such clairvoyants; few realize or recognize the differences in people and nearly all refuse to see what is unpleasant to look at. Few true clairvoyants admit their status or that they see more than others. There has been no significant contribution to the descriptions of thoughtforms since Charles Leadbeater and Annie Besant published their books early in this century. There was one significant contribution made by Madame Blavatsky in <u>Old Diary Leaves</u> which we have reproduced here with Leadbeater's comments and our own.

This is a fair copy of Madame Blavatsky's precipitation on silk of the aura of Mr. Stainton Moseyn. Mr. Moseyn was a high-grade disciple who contributed much in the early days of the Theosophical Society. In spite of the quality of the reproduction, there are a number of characteristics shown which our observations have confirmed:

1. The boiling, churning field and some indications of the "cage."

2. The unusually well-developed heart center located on the surface of the dark background of thoughtforms.

From *Old Diary Leaves*, Volume 1, page 364, by Colonel Olcott.

DIAGRAM 15

3. The presence of solar prana or vital force indicated by scattered points of light.

4. Conventionalized radiations from the heart and head centers.

5. An Earth energy, the apas tattva, shown in small wave-like forms.

This picture appears in <u>Old Diary Leaves,</u> Volume I, page 364, by Colonel Olcott and provides a typical example of the inner appearance of an advanced disciple, then and now.

In <u>The Masters and the Path,</u> page 118, C. W. Leadbeater comments on his illustrations of the astral and mental bodies of men at various stages of their progress as given in his earlier book, <u>Man, Visible and Invisible.</u> He states that,

> Those illustrations, however, gave only the exterior appearance of those bodies. . . . there is always a large portion in each vehicle which is not yet vivified—a heavy core which takes almost no part in the outer activities of the vehicle, and is indeed but little moved by them. But though this mass of comparatively inert matter is scarcely influenced by the more awakened portion, it is quite capable of acting upon the latter in certain ways. . . .
>
> This lethargic mass of unillumined matter has a certain life and tendencies of its own, which assert themselves when the more active part of the personality is somewhat in abeyance. . . . These qualities naturally vary with different people, but an intense egotism is almost always prominent. The thoughts and impressions generated by this sluggish kernel are often those of conceit and self-glorification, and also of instinctive self-preservation in the presence of any danger, whether real or imaginary. . . . There is a long period of slow unfoldment during which this heavy core is being gradually permeated by the light, being warmed and thawed into glowing response.

Students should have no difficulty in relating these quotations to what they are learning about the thoughtforms which, indeed, act along the lines indicated by Mr. Leadbeater. Note that he says the outer layers are activated first. He also says, "In some exalted moment an inrush of power from the ego may temporarily raise the standard of the personality, while on the other hand a steady pressure from the unused portion of the astral or mental body may for the time appreciably lower it."

We have said that, while the thoughtforms exist, downpours of energy from the Soul are deflected by them. Mr. Leadbeater either did not exactly identify what he saw or thought it inadvisable to describe it more fully. He does note that these sluggish portions in the aura are a very bad influence. He speaks of the "glowing response" when these negative factors are permeated by the light; we say that the imprisoned energy is redeemed or liberated. We also call your attention to the fact that the response of old thoughtforms is often far from "sluggish." Mr. Leadbeater has said nothing about the rather specific origin of thoughtforms, nor given anything but the vaguest suggestion as to their elimination. We have found that these thoughtforms *can* be eliminated by the processes outlined in this book.

THE NATURE OF THOUGHTFORMS

According to higher analysis, the lower vehicles (physical-etheric, emotional and mental) are all composed of gradations of spirit-matter of the lower planes. Everything that reaches man's consciousness on these levels, as he shapes his thoughtforms, goes into their structure. This means mental, astral, etheric and physical impressions, memories of all kinds and currents of mass thinking.

The energy-substance of the bewildering, deceiving, illusory nature of these thoughtforms is compressed into a confining layer of material. Therefore, the figments of one's own thinking, the false notions, the distorted and outgrown ideals constitute an obstruction and hindrance which veils the truth and shuts a man off from direct experience and knowledge of inner reality.

These contaminations affect a person in many ways. They stand like a network between him and his environment and interfere with true communication. On the receptive side, they channel mass consciousness, influence and suggestion, control by others, infection and disease. On the transmitting side, they cause self-depreciation and failure, excessive emotional reactions, misinterpretation of codes and conventions, undesirable behavior and imperfect response.

The ancient impurities—condensed thoughtforms carried over from life to life—stand between the person and his higher self and cause him to:

1. Hold to outworn and outgrown ideals;

2. Be deceived as to sources of inspiration;

3. Accept false teaching as true;

4. Misinterpret codes, customs and conven-

tions;

5. Make the techniques of Yoga and magic un-
successful and dangerous;

6. Prevent successful work with the glamors.

CREATION OF THOUGHTFORMS

Man's capacity to create began with his individualization eighteen million years ago. It was
then that animal-man was given the spark of
mind. However, man's undisciplined use of the
creative energy of the developing mental body
resulted in the creation of many undesirable
thoughtforms. The legened of Prometheus
bringing to man the fire of creation illustrates this
fact. This fire of mind given by Prometheus, the
Soul, must be tamed by the hard discipline of the
Law of Karma. Thus Prometheus (the Soul) was
chained to the rock (symbolizing matter) until this
control of the mind, and purification of matter,
was complete.

In the analysis of thoughtforms retained in the
electromagnetic field of a student, it is well to
note that the creation of such forms follows the
basic rule—a higher impulse acts upon a lower
(energy-matter) substance and produces an intermediate form or consciousness. The retained
thoughtforms, common to all, are kept because
the creative impulse was not strong enough to
project them outside the aura or electromagnetic
field to accomplish a visualized purpose, and the
created form remained attached to the creator to

be a continuing influence. Thoughtforms consist, therefore, of an impulsing energy holding matter-substance into a specific form, however imperfect. The following words are often used to define the steps of materialization:

IDEA   IDEAL   IDOL
ABSTRACT CONCRETE MATERIALIZATION

This outline is, of course, much too general. However, it indicates a basic truth concerning creation. That is that true creation requires the ability to contact the three higher levels of the mental plane (the abstract mind) where the Soul dwells. Ultimately, the Soul will absorb the four lower levels or subplanes comprising the concrete mind of the personality.* True creation begins with *ideas* which are to be found on some level of the abstract or higher mind. It is generally said that this level is formless, but since consciousness cannot exist without that spirit-matter combination which we have called form, there are forms. We point out that the concrete mind cannot create—it can only group or reassemble elements to be found on the various sublevels of all personality vehicles.

This reassembling process varies according to the matter of the subplane involved. For example, the lowest level of the mental plane responds to instinctual stimulus. Consequently, thoughtforms relating to sense impressions on

---

*For more information regarding the absorption of the personality by the Soul, see Esoteric Healing, by Alice A. Bailey, page 515, where Dwal Khul speaks about the elimination of the personality thoughtform.

the physical plane take shape. The second level responds to impacts of desire and emotion, which color and shape the thoughtforms formed there. The third subplane relates to mental impacts; consequently, thoughtforms on that level relate to mental attitudes concerning the two lower groups of thoughtforms.

The appearance of the fields and the relationship between the typical groups of thoughtforms and their location as to the body conforms to the three basic elements or mental subplane influences.

When the fourth subplane, the central subplane, comes into activity, the influence of the Soul is added to the material of the lower subplanes and the conflict accelerates.

Mistaken Creations

The condition of the planet and humanity today tells us forcibly that the purer ideas on Soul levels are not precipitated on the physical plane without incorrect modifications by spiritually undeveloped personalities.

It is asked how mistaken creations are possible, since all *true creation* begins with ideas on Soul levels. It must be sadly recognized that there are embodied forces which oppose the evolution of humanity and their influence accounts for most of the sorry history and constant conflict, both individual and collective.

The pure ideas of the Soul are presented on the

plane of the concrete mind by the Brothers of
Light and Great Teachers and teachings attest to
this. These adapted ideas, called ideals,[†] await
the disciple when consciousness rises to the
mental plane. It is the mistaken applications of
such ideals that impel the undesirable thoughtform creation, largely due to impacts from negative and evil sources.

When Soul influence takes over (in complete
control after the Third Initiation), mistaken creations are neutralized and the Soul can create the
ideals of the New Age without opposition. The
work outlined in this book will help the disciple
begin to create as a Soul.

Creation - Duration

To deal with the creation of thoughtforms, it is
necessary to give some consideration to the
nature of the mental plane itself in relation to the
influences of the past (karma) and the desired
future. The step-by-step process from the Soul
level (idea) to the materialization on the physical
plane is dealt with under the heading "Fifteen
Rules of Magic" in a brief form in A Treatise on
Cosmic Fire, and in the entire book, A Treatise
on White Magic. However, it is necessary that

[†]   An example of the relationship between ideas and
thought-forms on the lower levels of the mental plane is the
relationship of the idea which we call "chair." This could be
called an idea of support with no particular form. When that
idea is presented to the concrete mind it can gather the visible elements of that state of consciousness and present a
form which can be materialized in the thousand and one
forms which the idea of chair or support can take.

we deal with these subjects in a very compact and abbreviated form which may be far from satisfactory to the deeper investigator to whom we recommend a study of the sources we have mentioned.

A consideration of the relationship between duration and time as represented by Diagram 6 points out that *all creation is done in duration and that is where thoughtforms are built—on the lower mental plane.* Duration, in an absolute sense, is a quality of God and is therefore a timeless state. The best example of the relation of consciousness to duration is in the appreciation of music. Since music is based on sound, it requires a sequence of vibrations. Our senses "blur" that which is past with that to come and we apprehend in timeless duration.

All manifestation produces conditions in time and space which are relative to duration. The diagram shows duration extending into the past and future to different degrees, depending upon focus on the various planes and the relative density of the forms therein. In other words, duration for the Logos is without end, as depicted in Diagram 6, but duration as far as the concrete mind is concerned is relatively brief— like "seconds" to the Logos. Yet, in that area of duration, we have a certain measure of timelessness. It is as if the focus of creative thought requires that various elements of the past be combined with projections and recombinations determined by the intent, the Will or the desire of the creator. Until precipitated, karma is a record

of the past which, under the Law, will auto-
matically influence the creations which it is
desired to project into the future. The perception
of these influences of the past is not normally
developed enough to reveal them, but many elements are visible when clairvoyance is developed.

We may have no choice as to the general plan
of evolution, but we do have choice on the level
of the concrete mind, which is the level where, by
our acts of causation, we produce effects which
we call good or bad, and experience the results of
the effects and thereby learn wisdom which
reflects itself back to an effort to make our
choices creative and in line with the intention of
the Logos of this planet. This is control of the
future by its creation in duration, by the concrete
mind, with the assistance of the devas.[‡]

HORIZONTAL AND VERTICAL ACTIVATION

In order for existing thoughtforms, good or
bad, to be activated, there must be some kind of
stimulation. Once stimulated, these thoughtforms take on a life force of their own, affecting
a man's reactions to and perceptions of all that
surrounds him. The usual type of stimulation
which comes from sense impressions and contact

[‡] It has not been customary to emphasize the part played by the
devas prior to their release in 1975. The devic substance of the
mental plane may respond directly to the Will of man, but the
cooperation of greater devas is now given to disciples, particularly
those working with and for the program of the Christ and Hierarchy.

with the environment is a horizontal stimulation. Whatever has caused the stimulation contains an energy of a similar vibration to that of the thoughtform and begins to resonate with the thoughtform stimulating that which already exists. Every emotional *reaction* is an example of horizontal stimulation.

This horizontal stimulation is used by many psychologists in ingenuous and sometimes injurious efforts to eliminate the engrams or complexes (which they sense but cannot see) by having the disciple relive the experience which first caused the pattern or complex.* Horizontal stimulation is produced by activities which are identical or very similar to that which produced the original thoughtform and, such stimulation *adds energy to the original form.* The expenditure of energy may result in a feeling of temporary relief until the energy builds up again, but *does not eliminate the original thoughtform.* The activation enlarges the thoughtform which again condenses into an inactive condition until the next horizontal stimulation occurs.

In contrast to the normal horizontal (environmental) sense reactions, the thoughtform can be stimulated by a vertical (subjective) Soul-directed

---

*Dwal Khul has said that disciples should avoid psychologists because they do not understand disciples. However, today there are disciples who are psychologists and students who may find assistance, particularly those students who are still mystics and demand leaders. We suggest that those interested in psychological approaches begin with what Dwal Khul has said in Esoteric Psychology, Volume II, page 401. The solution to problems of this nature rests with the Soul and not on the level of the concrete mind.

corresponding energy which is drawn from the rainbow fire of the Central Channel and the Soul Star. This corresponding relationship between the spiritual energy used to remove the pattern and that contained in the pattern is analogous to the octaves on a piano; if one "C" is touched on the keyboard, all other "C's" on the piano vibrate. This Soul fire is of a greater intensity and higher frequency than that which originally produced the thoughtform. Consequently, there is a reaction to the impact of Soul energy through the voiced words and statements, and the thoughtform begins to expand and finally disintegrates. This vertical type of stimulation is the chief observation upon which our work is based.

ELIMINATION OF THOUGHTFORMS

All thoughtforms will *ultimately* return to the matter of which they were made, if not nourished or added to by the creative power of man. By using the higher energies of the Soul this process is greatly accelerated.

According to the Law of Karma, any cause will produce effects which stand as an incomplete record of purpose and activity until fulfilled as intended by precipitation into form. Since these thoughtforms represent karma to be worked out by the individual, the elimination of these forms from the field of the disciple can save lifetimes of incarnated effort. The processes of elimination described in this book justify our statement that karma *can* be changed or neutralized. The right

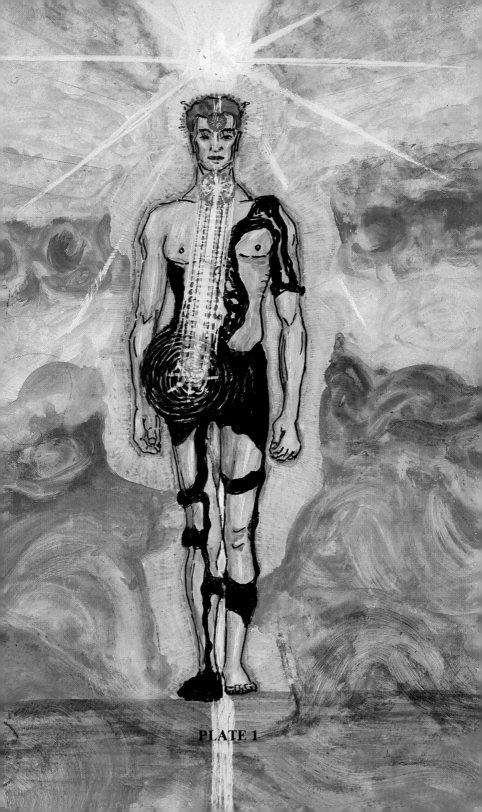

PLATE 1

The human animal made many mistakes in the creation of Gods and Devils, mostly in his own image, but sometimes as distortions of the devic forms of natural forces.

PLATE 2

Do not be concerned that there has been evil in your ancient past. It is the same with all. Be grateful that by the Grace of God you can destroy the last record.

PLATE 3

PLATE 4

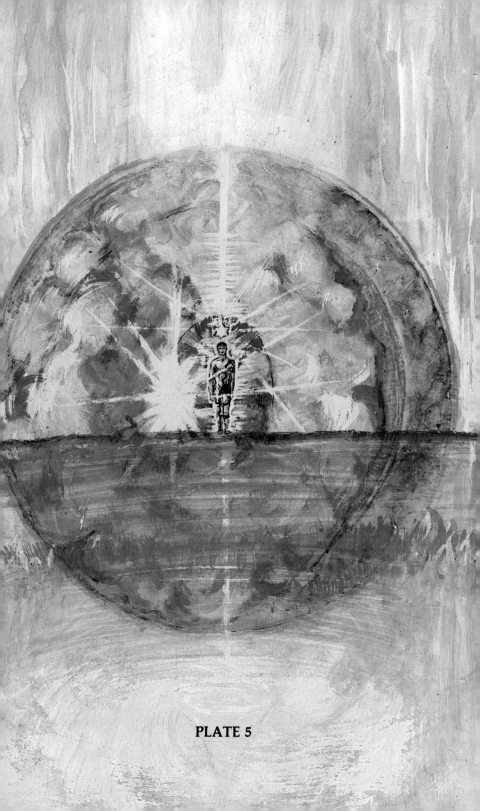

PLATE 5

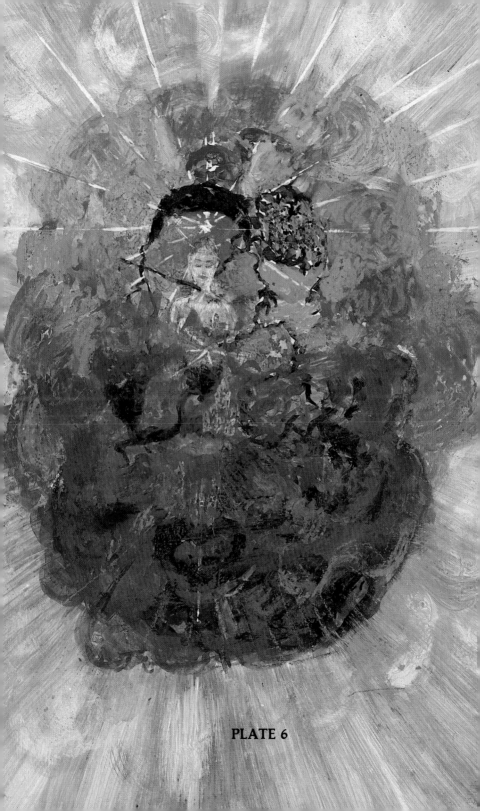

PLATE 6

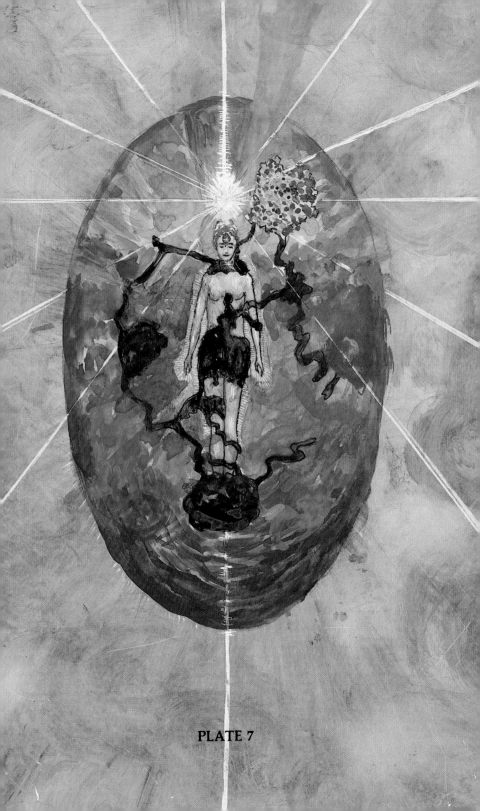

PLATE 7

PLATE 8

techniques, in combination with the power of the Soul, can cause these thoughtforms to disintegrate and disappear, releasing creative energy to be stored in the Causal field. By using a higher energy, the energy of the Soul, the thoughtforms can be eliminated, karma offset and the disciple freed to be of greater service and usefulness. †

Much has been written and poured over by students, and the accumulation of knowledge *about* occult subjects has not lessened the accumulation of hindrances to spiritual progress. The attempts at techniques of yoga, prayer, affirmation, invocation, use of the sacred word, etc. are relatively useless by comparison to those same techniques practiced by disciples free of the observable hindrances and obstacles (which clutter the auras of all spiritual teachers we have seen). Even more futile are the attempts of self-styled teachers to "clear" or do the work *for* others which those others must do for themselves; this is esoteric law.

The statement has been made that the Soul knows no evil. How then can the Soul relate to thoughtforms which may be powerfully evil, such as the satyr form which is shown in color plate number 2, which appears in the fields of many disciples during activation of thoughtforms, obviously relating to sex and violence. There are many nymphs and satyrs and un-

†This clearing has been done in the past in Ashrams or retreats, under controlled environment between the Second and Third Initiations by Initiates or Masters. This avoids the horizontal activation which disciples "in the world" cannot easily avoid.

imaginable monstrosities somewhere in our past, most of which are grossly sexual with distortions such as medieval artists pictured indirectly from clairvoyant observation.

The fact is that what is "evil" is the misuse of creative energy, the same creative energy which could have been used for good creations, which means that the matter gathered to produce the evil form was of low grade, heavy quality, governed by instincts and/or desires and selfishness generally.

But for every manifestation on the levels of personality life, there is a corresponding reality on Soul levels. There is always a true idea on the levels of the abstract mind which is in back of the mental forms existing on lower levels.

Energy itself is impersonal, it goes where it is sent (energy follow thought). This gift of creative thought was released for man to learn how to use it correctly which so often results in painful mistakes. But in the end we all learn and when we again invite the higher creative energy into the same area of thought, with the firm motivation of doing it right this time, then the heavier material of the form cannot hold together under the steadier high vibration and dissolves into its primal unformed substance. If the higher energy is continued, the freed creative energy is increased in a downpour of the pure Soul energy, and can be used *for higher purposes.* If not so used, it goes into the Causal field and remains as a reservoir of power or may be used to begin the building of the Body of Light. The personality has nothing whatever to do with this creation which follows an archetype controlled by Hierarchy.

When pure Soul energy, evoked by the *sound* of the words and phrases, mantrams or invocations, is attracted by synchronous vibration into contact with the thoughtform, it is immediately activated. The vibration of the thoughtform is intensified by the directed energy of the Soul, tuned into the thoughtform through the basic idea, intensified to a point where the thoughtform cannot retain its structure and is disintegrated into the basic elements of which it was composed. If the activation is not promptly followed by another Soul instrument, the spiritual vortex, it begins to take form and the destruction is more difficult. We refer to the series of color plates which illustrates the process as seen by clairvoyant observation.

Since the obstructions described are *forms* which must be destroyed, the First Ray[‡] aspects of Soul Energy (the energies of the Soul Star and the Central Channel in their power aspect) must be called upon by *invocation of the Soul,* the *fixed determination* of the student, *persistence* and *concentration*—all of which are techniques by which the personal self calls in Soul energy.

The process of removing thoughtforms is also a form of intelligent activity (a Third Ray acti-

---

[‡] We refer students to the tabulation of the Rays and their corresponding qualities, which is in this book under the section, "Planes and Rays."

vity). After the Soul Star has been activated by the use of the Soul Mantram, spiritual energy begins to flow down through the Central Channel and is deflected in a ray of light through the throat center, the clearest of the substitute centers in the majority of people. (See Color Plate 1.) The ray from the throat center seeks out the pattern or patterns containing a similar frequency and impacts the pattern or thoughtform until there is a disintegration of the pattern, releasing the energy contained within it and destroying the magnetic substance that had held it in form. Both the energy thus released and the substance or etheric matter from the disintegrated thoughtform must be removed by using the Whirlwind or vortex. (See Color Plates 3 and 4.) The lowest and heaviest energy-substance is thus removed by the use of the vortex; the higher energies remain in the Causal field. (See Color Plate 5.) It is necessary to remind the student that the energy-substance being broken up may not and probably is not related to *present* life activities or express *present* development, conditions or activity.

It should be noted that no concentration upon the throat center is required or desirable; the energy and center is used and controlled by the Soul's activity. It is pointed out that, at this time, the center referred to is the sensitized point developed during the building of the Central Channel and is *not* the major center itself, which the Soul will develop and position when it is possible to do so, once the body is freed from hindering thoughtforms.

EXPLANATION OF COLOR PLATES

When we first began our experiments on clearing, we kept detailed records. Among them are the few color plates in this book and the picture of the cleared field on the back cover.

The first five plates are a series showing the activation of an instinctual thoughtform. The last three plates are a series indicating points of development in the clearing process.

Picture Number One: Activation

The invoked energy of the Soul passes through the throat center and is directed to the portion of condensed thoughtforms which corresponds in frequency to the energies in the word used in the line form. In this particular case, the energies corresponded to patterns located over the right groin area. In this plate the pattern begins to expand once it is activated by the impact of Soul energy.

Picture Number Two: Precipitation

The physical-etheric, astral and mental matter assumes the shape built into it when the thoughtform was originally created. Satyrs and nymphs were common thoughtforms, created in the ancient time when such animal forms existed. This particular thoughtform, once activated, appeared very threatening, growling and snarling and offensive smelling.

Picture Number Three: Invocation of Vortex

After allowing formation of this old image relating to sex and violence, we invoked the spiritual vortex which descended as shown in this plate. As it touched the figure, the pattern "froze" and did not move thereafter.

Picture Number Four: The Break-Up

Once the vortex hit the thoughtform it disintegrated, releasing red and green energies which went into the Causal Field, while the gross matter of the form descended into the lower portion of the field to be swept into the etheric fires of the Earth by the descending vortices.

Picture Number Five: The Final Blast

The intensity of the activating Soul energy grew more and more pronounced until the remaining dark mass exploded into light and the resultant red and green energies were released from the disintegration of the form.

Although some students objected to our showing such malevolent forms as they appeared, there were also angelic figures, thoughtforms of Masters, and simulated God figures, all creations of the past. The student should not identify these evoked thoughtforms from the past with the present life, nor should the student be disturbed by them. More advanced work by students will include elimination of accumulations of this type on a planetary scale. The destruction of these forms should not be regretted. They are of the past and represent *outworn* ideals and beliefs. The good in

them is built into Soul consciousness even though
the form is destroyed.

Pictures Number Six, Seven and Eight

Taken as a series, these plates show the progres-
sion of the individual's clearing. Plate 6 shows
how most people look before they have done any
clearing work. Loose debris has accumulated in
their fields, the result of environmental contact.
The cage is built around them and the external
patterns cling to the body. Only a glimmer of the
Soul Star's radiation is visible through these
accumulations.

Plate 7 shows partial clearing of the field with
the fogs and miasmas gone and parts of the cage
still remaining. This individual still has the external thoughtforms which adhere to the body.

Plate 8 shows the cleared fields of an individual
who has completed the Phase II work. The external patterns adhering to the body are gone, the
Soul Star is very strong and the Central Channel is
well defined. The health aura is not inhibited by
adhering thoughtforms. The astral and larger
mental bodies are clear but unorganized. The
centers are shown as minor centers, which is usual
at this stage of evolution. The Causal Field, in the
background, is very large and is filled with
various energies which have accumulated during
the clearing processes as a reservoir of power.
What is shown in this plate can be achieved from
between two to five years, depending upon the
persistence, concentration and Soul response of
the disciple.

ELIMINATION TECHNIQUES

Persistent application of the techniques to be given here will enable the student to clear away the obstructing thoughtforms and fill the field and inner vehicles with radiant spiritual energy.

It is helpful, but not necessary, to work with another student when clearing away the thoughtforms; many have successfully done the work alone. The following form is suggested when doing the clearing work:

1. Say the Soul Mantram:

> I am the Soul.
> I am the Light Divine.
> I am Love.
> I am Will.
> I am Fixed Design.

No work will be effective without cooperation from the Soul.

2. Take the Soul Star from its position above the head to the point below the feet, thinking of it spinning from left to right (clockwise), and bring it rapidly up the Central Channel. This will clear and gradually enlarge the channel. Follow with the spiritual vortex.

3. Link mentally by projecting a line of light to the Group Soul of the parent (Prototype) group, to its teachers who authored *The Rainbow Bridge,* to the several Associate Groups and their members, to any other persons working with the Phase I and II techniques whom you may know,

and to the New Group of World Servers, generally. See these connecting lines of light on the astral and mental planes as well.

    4. Say the Mantram of Unification:

> "The sons of men are one
> and I am one with them.
> I seek to love, not hate;
> I seek to serve and not exact due service;
> I seek to heal, not hurt.

> Let pain bring due reward of light and love.
> Let the Soul control the outer form
> and life and all events,
> And bring to light the love which underlies
> the happenings of the time.

> Let vision come and insight.
> Let the future stand revealed.
> Let inner union demonstrate and
> outer cleavages be gone.
> Let love prevail.
> Let all men love."

Of this Mantram the Tibetan Master, Dwal Khul, has said:

> These words may seem inadequate, but said with power and an understanding of their significance and with the potency of the mind and heart behind them, they can prove unbelievably potent in the life of the one who says them. They will produce also an effect in his environment, and the accumulated effects in the world, as you spread the knowledge of the formula, will be great and effective. It will change attitudes, enlighten the vision and lead the aspirant to fuller service and to a wider cooperation

based upon sacrifice. My brothers, you cannot
evade the sacrifice in the long run, even if you
have evaded it until now.[§]

This Mantram is a modernized and mystically
worded version of the one which was used widely
in Atlantean days during the period of the
ancient conflict of which the present is an effect.

5. Do the word form or line work for five to
seven minutes to activate the thoughtform. *There
is a time factor here which must be observed.* The
line work must be continued until the disintegration of the thoughtform stops. It has been observed that the average time required for this
activation is from five to seven minutes. Until the
inner vision or knowing develops in the student,
the time required should be sensed by the student
insofar as is possible, but activation should be
continued by the clock until enough sensitivity is
developed to know inwardly when it is complete.

6. Then use the spiritual vortex to clear away
the debris left from the disintegrated pattern.
The vortex should be invoked and visualized with
the creative imagination for six to eight minutes,
carrying it deep into the Earth.

Start out by doing one line a day; increase to
two lines after one week. The fourth week
increase to four lines a day if you can spare the
time to do so. Do not strain at the work. More
hours spent do not achieve proportionate results.
Be consistent, but not fanatic.

[§]Externalization of the Hierarchy, by Alice A. Bailey, page 142.

7. Close your work by saying The Great Invocation:

"From the point of Light within the Mind of God
Let Light stream forth into the minds of men.
Let Light descend on Earth.

From the point of Love within the Heart of God
Let Love stream forth into the hearts of men.
May Christ return to Earth.

From·the center where the Will of God is known
Let purpose guide the little wills of men—
The purpose which the Masters know and serve.

From the center which we call the race of men
Let the Plan of Love and Light work out.
And may it seal the door where evil dwells.

Let Light and Love and Power restore the Plan on Earth."

The Line Forms

The thoughtforms have been created by your past thinking, feeling, action, activities—all of your past—for they are carried over from life to life as seeds in your permanent atoms and activated horizontally by circumstances and karma in this life. They relate to contact and relationship of two basic activities which we have called the horizontal and vertical relationships. The horizontal activation relates to your recognized and conscious form-contacts, though you do not remember them in terms of sense perception records of what happened in other lives.

The vertical relates to your unconscious contacts, both with your higher self or Soul and your submerged or unconscious self—that which is *above* or *below* the present threshold of consciousness. Then relationships can be expressed symbolically and diagrammatically as follows:

SELF   —   NOT SELF
or
"I"   "U"

The application of these terms is very flexible. "I" is your present focus of consciousness. "U" is *everything* else.

What "I" is is determined by your development and choice, that is, what you identify with. You can say "I suffer" or "I enjoy" and refer to and identify with sensation or body, in which case the body or vehicle is included as "I." Or you can say "I am the Soul" and begin to be the *observer* of bodies and sensations of the "U." If you try to discover what and where the "I" is, you will probably retreat to a point back of the eyes—for which the anatomists have searched in vain—although in some cases the pineal gland is considered as the location of the "I." Of course, the "I" is not in physical form and never will be. It is the One Life, focused and limited temporarily by some form, and this is why we say "the application is flexible" depending on time, space, circumstance and form. When you refer to the Self as "I" *after identification with the Soul,* the Soul will make the proper application according to the word or words used.

We have divided the "I" and "U" into

conscious and sub- and super-conscious factors
—calling them "I," "U," and Self or mySelf.

Although identification is fluid and determined by the Soul at the Center, we assume that
"I" is your present consciousness, limited in
many ways but looking to the Soul at the Center
to direct the energies specifically.

As can be seen from the above depiction of the
line structure, the word forms are divided into
three basic aspects: horizontal, vertical, and
internal.* Horizontal refers to the relationship
between "I" and "U." Vertical refers to the
relationship between "I" and "mySelf."

---

*Students may recognize the "I" and "U" as the self and not-self of
older teachings. See Diagram 16 for the relationship of "self" to "I" to
"you."

Internal refers to the relationship between "U" and "mySelf." You cannot use this "U"-"mySelf" aspect effectively for a long time, so we shall not explain it further at this time. The first two aspects are all that are needed to handle external images or thoughtforms.

Each set of lines contains two parts divided into four sections each, for a total of sixty-four lines. The design of each set of eight lines is easily memorized. The line forms should be studied and the relationships understood. The first half of each line is always the same in each set. The last half of the line states the relationship involved in reference to the first half but follows the same general design. The first half relates to the *desire* nature, the second half relates to *action,* and voicing the line to achieve purification and redemption of the spiritual energy locked in the patterns, represents *intention.* These three aspects— *intention, desire, action*— reflect the trinity of Life, Consciousness, and Form.

Words

It would be hard to find a quotation which has more concealed in it or one which needs more interpretation than the following one from A Treatise on Cosmic Fire, page 452, concerning words:

> The "Words" are used for the manipulation of
> matter and its bending into form along the line
> of evolution. Until the inner faculty of clair-
> voyance is somewhat developed, this know-

ledge of mantrams remains practically useless
and may be even a menace. When a man can see
a need for correction and for adjustment in a
brother's vehicle, and can awaken in his
brother a desire to adjust that which is amiss,
wise assistance can be given by the one who sees
and sounds. Think this out, for it holds the key
to the reason for the safeguarding of the words.

Selflessness, sight, and sincerity of purpose
must all three exist before the sounds can be
imparted. Selflessness and sincerity are sometimes found but the occult use of the inner
vision is still rare.

The word forms in our work not only *activate*
but also *limit* the area of activation. The second
function is probably more important than the
first because the removal of thoughtforms must
be gradual to be *safe*. At first, such is the general
nature of the image complexes that there are
many words or word combinations that would
serve. However, a series of lines has been
adopted, embodying the word forms, covering
most human relationships to be used until the
outer cage and many of the mass of thoughtforms adhering to the body are gone.

The sequence of descent from *sound* to *the
word*, to *words* and *languages* is suggested in
Diagram 16. Since the Soul works with *ideas* and
not languages, the original language which pre-
vailed when the thoughtform was made is of little
or no importance.

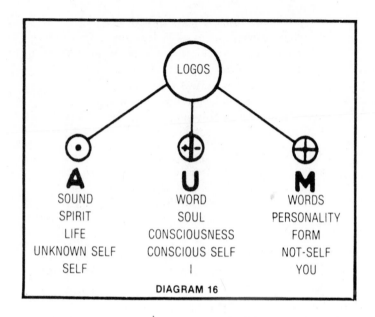

DIAGRAM 16

We have not found it necessary to use the AUM in the conventional way since its effectiveness is dependent upon the development of the disciple. As a symbol it is the summation of all the sounds of speech and the sound will therefore vary according to racial variations in body and head structure.

Since the Sacred Word contains all sounds, *all words are part of it and therefore all words are sacred according to the purpose and energy which they carry.* YOU MUST USE THE LINES WITH THIS IN MIND. There is an etheric sound back of the physical vibration of air which is not limited by the air or physical voice.§

----

§"... the words spoken by ... every individual largely determine his future fate ... because ... when our soul (mind) creates or evokes a thought, the representative sign of that thought is self-

The basic words to use in the lines are:

First Set	Second Set	Third Set
1. do	13. act	25. think
2. have	14. stand	26. persist
3. be	15. accept	27. conceive
4. perceive	16. reject	28. catalog
5. love	17. divide	29. analyze
6. know	18. blend	30. unify
7. go	19. move	31. express
8. stay	20. hold	32. preserve
9. give	21. attract	33. invoke
10. receive	22. repulse	34. formulate
11. separate	23. isolate	35. renounce
12. merge	24. fuse	36. integrate

In addition to the above, the following five words have proved very effective and can be used more than once:

1. balance
2. align
3. change
4. adapt
5. communicate

As to the words themselves, it is obvious that special study could be given to their choice and

---

engraved upon the astral fluid, which is the receptacle and, so to say, the mirror of all the manifestations of being. . . . To pronounce a word is to evoke a thought, and make it present; the magnetic potency of human speech is the commencement of every manifestation in the Occult World." The Secret Doctrine, Volume I, by H. P. Blavatsky, pages 120-121. All occult techniques emphasize the need to control speech, even to the extent of enforced silence for two years in the Platonic School. *The real potency of the word is in its immovable or silent aspect.*

sequence. †The sets we have suggested came from our own study and experience; that is, we chose the words which were most effective in activating old thoughtforms. In this experience with ourselves and some others we took note of:

1. The quickness and intensity of activation.

2. The energy colors involved.

3. Reactions of the centers.

4. Nature of the debris from disintegration.

5. Any forms evoked, which told us often of the physical life situation, action or habits involved in the original construction or growth.

6. The time required to activate and clear.

7. Finally, the Soul energy which was available after the removal of obstacles, hindrances and obstructions.

It will be noticed that all of these words are "action words," verbs, which fall into the basic categories of action, desire and being. Some action—physical, emotional or mental—lies back of the creation of the thoughtforms you will now begin to remove.

These lines can be done under almost any conditions and in any position that does not interfere with reasonable concentration. The pri-

†Do not use negative words such as "hate," "fear," "loss," etc. The Soul only reacts to abstract ideas of positive realities. The negative words sometimes evoke the positive ones, but there seems to be unnecessary delay and uncertainty in this procedure.

mary requirement is attention, which if wandering or uncertain can be brought back to focus upon the word being used through the use of the lines. Sleepiness or wandering thoughts will interfere with concentration, but a consistent returning to the lines will correct this in time.

The line should be said aloud once and then said silently or mentally twice, repeating this until from five to seven minutes have passed, or until activation ceases. Insert the first word "do" in the first line thus:

"I never desire to do anything for you and I always do everything for you."

Continue with the word "do" through all sixty-four lines before you go to the next word, "have," which you will use in all the lines before you go to the next word, "be," and so on, through all 36 words listed.

Once a line is activated for from five to seven minutes and cleared with the vortex or Whirlwind for from six to eight minutes, the line does not have to be repeated; the pattern related to it will have been removed in most instances. If activation was not complete, further activation will continue through the rest of the lines in the set being done, and will generally be cleared by the time the set has been completed. This is not an inflexible rule, however, because some words can be repeated many times with activation and clearing. Your observation of daily life experience should indicate whether you will need to repeat a word and portion of the line set.

The process of breaking up thoughtforms or image complexes and the cage is a transmutation process as well as a purification process. Through the impact of spiritual energy and the elimination of these forms, two products result: the "latent" energy liberated from the patterns is stored in the field—made available for higher uses; and the matter-substance which confined the energy in the thoughtform now is precipitated in the field as "ash," "fog," "dust," or some kind of debris. This latter substance-matter debris is undesirable to keep in the field because it would slowly be added to other existing thoughtforms. This debris should be cleared out of the electromagnetic field at once by use of the vortex for from six to eight minutes. If it is not removed immediately, it will sometimes take form as a scene, a person, a symbol, or some other form which students with slight clair-voyance may see. To some, this is frightening. But there is nothing to fear from such forms because they are not real, existing usually on the emotional or astral level of consciousness and easily removed with the vortex.

Too much significance should not be given to these specters of the past; they should be calmly observed and then swept away by the vortex. The substance thus eliminated from an individual, conditioned through human use, is carried down into the Earth where it becomes of use to lower kingdoms in nature—animal, vegetable, or mineral. Nothing is destroyed or lost, all in nature is recycled.

The Parts and sets of lines to be used are here given:

PART 1-A

1. I never desire to _____ anything _____ you and I always _____ everything _____ you.

2. You never desire to _____ anything _____ me and you always _____ everything _____ me.

3. I always desire to _____ everything _____ you and I never _____ anything _____ you.

4. You always desire to _____ everything _____ me and you never _____ anything _____ me.

5. I never desire to _____ anything _____ you and I never _____ anything _____ you.

6. You never desire to _____ anything _____ me and you never _____ anything _____ me.

7. I always desire to _____ everything _____ you and I always _____ everything _____ you.

8. You always desire to _____ everything _____ me and you always _____ everything _____ me.

PART 2-A

1. I never desire to ____ anything ____ mySelf
   and I always ____ everything ____ mySelf.

2. MySelf never desires to ____ anything ____ me
   and mySelf always ____ everything ____ me.

3. I always desire to ____ everything ____ mySelf
   and I never ____ anything ____ mySelf.

4. MySelf always desires to ____ everything ____
   me and mySelf never ____ anything ____ me.

5. I never desire to ____ anything ____ mySelf
   and I never ____ anything ____ mySelf.

6. MySelf never desires to ____ anything ____ me
   and mySelf never ____ anything ____ me.

7. I always desire to ____ everything ____ mySelf
   and I always ____ everything ____ mySelf.

8. MySelf always desires to ____ everything ____
   me and mySelf always ____ everything ____
   me.

PART 1-B

1. I never desire to ____ anything ____ you and you always ____ everything ____ me.

2. You never desire to ____ anything ____ me and I always ____ everything ____ you.

3. I always desire to ____ everything ____ you and you never ____ anything ____ me.

4. You always desire to ____ everything ____ me and I never ____ anything ____ you.

5. I never desire to ____ anything ____ you and you never ____ anything ____ me.

6. You never desire to ____ anything ____ me and I never ____ anything ____ you.

7. I always desire to ____ everything ____ you and you always ____ everything ____ me.

8. You always desire to ____ everything ____ me and I always ____ everything ____ you.

PART 2-B

1. I never desire to _____ anything _____ mySelf and mySelf always _____ everything _____ me.

2. MySelf never desires to _____ anything _____ me and I always _____ everything _____ mySelf.

3. I always desire to _____ everything _____ mySelf and mySelf never _____ anything _____ me.

4. MySelf always desires to _____ everything _____ me and I never _____ anything _____ mySelf.

5. I never desire to _____ anything _____ mySelf and mySelf never _____ anything _____ me.

6. MySelf never desires to _____ anything _____ me and I never _____ anything _____ mySelf.

7. I always desire to _____ everything _____ mySelf and mySelf always _____ everything _____ me.

8. MySelf always desires to _____ everything _____ me and I always _____ everything _____ mySelf.

PART 1-C

1. I never desire you to ____ anything ____ me and I always ____ everything ____ you.

2. You never desire me to ____ anything ____ you and you always ____ everything ____ me.

3. I always desire you to ____ everything ____ me and I never ____ anything ____ you.

4. You always desire me to ____ everything ____ you and you never ____ anything ____ me.

5. I never desire you to ____ anything ____ me and I never ____ anything ____ you.

6. You never desire me to ____ anything ____ you and you never ____ anything ____ me.

7. I always desire you to ____ everything ____ me and I always ____ everything ____ you.

8. You always desire me to ____ everything ____ you and you always ____ everything ____ me.

PART 2-C

1. I never desire mySelf to _____ anything _____ me
   and I always _____ everything _____ mySelf.

2. MySelf never desires me to _____ anything _____
   mySelf and mySelf always _____ everything
   _____ me.

3. I always desire mySelf to _____ everything _____
   me and I never _____ anything _____ mySelf.

4. MySelf always desires me to _____ everything
   _____ mySelf and mySelf never _____ anything
   _____ me.

5. I never desire mySelf to _____ anything _____ me
   and I never _____ anything _____ mySelf.

6. MySelf never desires me to _____ anything _____
   mySelf and mySelf never _____ anything _____
   me.

7. I always desire mySelf to _____ everything _____
   me and I always _____ everything _____
   mySelf.

8. MySelf always desires me to _____ everything
   _____ mySelf and mySelf always _____ everything _____ me.

PART 1-D

1. I always desire you to____everything____me
   and you never____anything____me.

2. You never desire me to ____ anything ____ you
   and I always ____ everything ____ you.

3. I always desire you to ____ everything ____ me
   and you never ____ anything ____ me.

4. You always desire me to ____ everything ____
   you and I never ____ anything ____ you.

5. I never desire you to ____ anything ____ me
   and you never ____ anything ____ me.

6. You never desire me to ____ anything ____ you
   and I never ____ anything ____ you.

7. I always desire you to ____ everything ____ me
   and you always ____ everything ____ me.

8. You always desire me to ____ everything ____
   you and I always ____ everything ____ you.

PART 2-D

1. I never desire mySelf to _____ anything _____ me
   and mySelf always _____ everything _____ me.

2. MySelf never desires me to _____ anything _____
   mySelf and I always _____ everything _____
   mySelf.

3. I always desire mySelf to _____ everything _____
   me and mySelf never _____ anything _____
   me.

4. MySelf always desires me to _____ everything
   _____ mySelf and I never _____ anything _____
   mySelf.

5. I never desire mySelf to _____ anything _____ me
   and mySelf never _____ anything _____ me.

6. MySelf never desires me to _____ anything _____
   mySelf and I never _____ anything _____
   mySelf.

7. I always desire mySelf to _____ everything _____
   me and mySelf always _____ everything _____
   me.

8. MySelf always desires me to _____ everything
   _____ mySelf and I always _____ everything
   _____mySelf.

These lines are not affirmations or denials in the mentalist sense as usually understood. The lines are generalized statements which, enunciated *as if the soul,* direct energies into the field of the personality. The cumulative effect of the impact of these energies is the gradual elimination of specific defects in the personality.

When a word is finally cleared, the seventh and eighth lines, the double positives, may be used like affirmations when needed. The result is an instantaneous downpour of Soul energy. The disciple must not neglect to use his gained capacities and the means of protection which are given later in this chapter.

Any preposition that makes the line meaningful to you may be used in the second blank of each line. With the first word, "do," the prepositions "for," "to," or "with" can be used with equal effect. Select the preposition (word of relationship) that suits you.

Often, there is an arrogance in concrete minds of a certain type, which immediately assumes that by some trick of words or attitudes a cautious approach is not necessary; that elimination can be made almost instantaneously. A number of students make experiments against all instructions; this is not as serious in the first phase work, but can be deadly when it comes to the second phase, particularly when combined with partial knowledge of energies, centers, forces and so on, concerning patterns.*

It should be pointed out that our work is designed to produce *safe results*. The grammatical structure and specific meanings of the lines limit and control the range of the activation energies. Thus, the process is "graded, guarded and guided" to effect Soul-controlled results.

The disciple *should not focus on the centers or chakras*. While the body contains patterns and obstructing thoughtforms, activation of the centers can cause great damage to the vehicles. Once activated, the centers begin the process of elimination. This proceeds too fast for the body to handle the debris and can be fatal to the physical vehicles. This we know from our own experience. When the centers are ready to be safely activated, *the Soul* proceeds to do so.

Therefore, the work must be done gradually. Persistent application to the clearing work will result in real gains for the disciple, and is far more effective than the fanatical attempts to clear the vehicles "all at once." Remember, the Soul is doing this clearing work so that It can have a more receptive vehicle for expression of Soul energy on the physical plane.

*There are those who object to the pointing out of dangers in occult work. They need to be reminded that to compress thousands of years of normal evolution into a few years, or even lifetimes, requires effort, some danger, and above all, *endurance*.

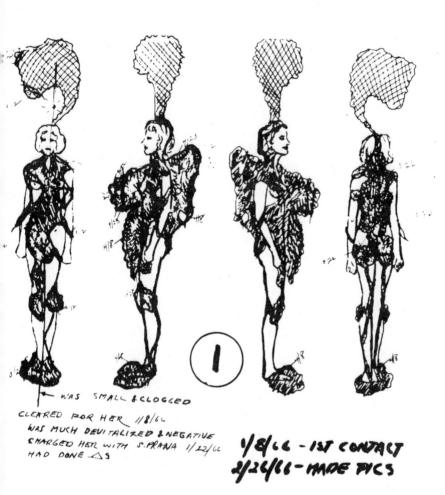

WAS SMALL & CLOGGED

CLEARED FOR HER 1/8/66
WAS MUCH DEVITALIZED & NEGATIVE
CHARGED HER WITH S. PRANA 1/22/66
HAD DONE △s

1/8/66 - 1ST CONTACT
2/26/66 - MADE PICS

The full-sized sheet marked Number One, and Number
Two and Three on the next page, are pictures in a series
showing the beginning and end of the external patterns and
thoughtforms which are removed in Phase II. The pictures
are a form of "stenography" which was devised to record
the progress of the elimination process. In Number One,
the record was made in January 1966. Such records, shown
here for most of our founding group, were kept in detail.
We continued keeping records of this type until we were in-

(Continued next page)

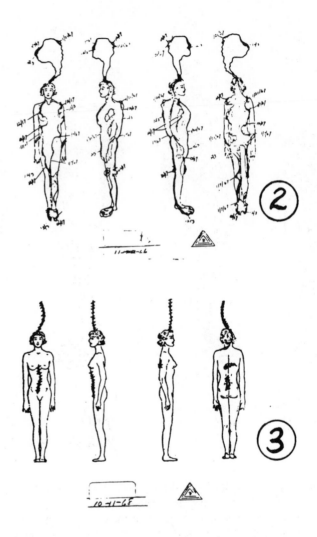

structed that they were not necessary. The dates marked on
the outside of the patterns in Number One were drawn to
show what had been eliminated since the last picture was
made. The process was completed with this particular disciple on October 11, 1968, and her field then resembled that on
the back cover of this book.

BEING THE OBSERVER

The lines are keys which unlock karmic residue so that Soul energy can destroy the old forms and redeem the energy locked up in them—that same energy which impels the student into emotional turmoil and mental confusion or stress. Thus, the Phase II process is a way in which karma can be changed without "living it out"—and we know of no other way.

Since the clearing work of Phase II is aimed at breaking up the ancient thoughtforms and destroying them with Soul energy rather than living out the karma which they represent, the disciple undertaking this work is subjecting himself to a *forcing process* by consciously determining to do that which is the Will of the Soul. Consequently, situations and relationships which are an obstacle to growth are brought to the forefront and examined in the Light of the Soul.

The changing events of the disciple's life should be *observed*. Many occurrences and periods of crisis are transitory in nature and once experienced provide the disciple with more strength and insight, leaving him better equipped to handle his affairs.

The *observer* is the Soul in the first manifestation of fusion. By being the Observer you identify yourself with the Soul. What is observed, however, is not always pleasing, for often it is recognized failure to live up to the highest; often it is pain; too often a deadly recognition of past wrong action producing present disaster. Sometimes, in relation to others, we find that we are unreasonably condemning ourselves with a false sense of responsibility for their actions. This is particularly true of most parents' attitudes about their grown children. Observe quietly, amid the storm, and say "suffer it to be so now," knowing that a new day will bring the Sun of understanding and the light which will show the way.

The Brothers have told us that in the past the clearing processes have been done in Ashrams or controlled environments and have been available only to Second Degree Initiates. Disciples undertaking this work of purification, however, must live in the world and contend with the daily demands and contacts of personality life.

The Path is not easy and is not usually undertaken until the disciple has exhausted all need of human experience and is oriented to progress in subjective matters and spiritual realities generally. This occurs when the long series of incarnations are near the end, when successes and failures are registered in the capacities of the Soul and no longer are needed for the development of love and wisdom. All who are a part of that band of disciples, the New Group of World Servers, are on that Path which leads "from darkness into Light, from the unreal to the Real, from death to Immortality."

DEVELOPING SENSITIVITY
TO FREQUENCIES

Energy is a synthetic term—as white is a synthetic color. Within the color we call white all other colors of the spectrum are to be found; this fact is easily demonstrated by passing a beam of white light through a prism. Each color in the spectrum represents a frequency, a characteristic vibration, but it is known that this band of color extends in both directions beyond the visible spectrum and that it expresses in related frequency intervals or modulations. The energies we come to recognize and use are of this nature and could be termed "ultra-high frequencies," the spiritual energies. As a start, however, we visualize the colors of the known spectrum and begin to identify and sense the inherent energy frequency that shows itself in the form of color and light.

Using the mental tools of visualization and imagination, students may begin to sharpen sensitivity to the different frequencies by centering attention (concentration) in the Soul Star and drawing forth from its brilliant synthetic white light the selected color. For example, draw forth from the center of the Soul Star a stream of the beautiful violet light, directing it to flow downward through the body to bathe every cell and then to fill the energy structures surrounding the body. The violet light in its lowest and most familiar aspect or octave is the ultra-violet light used as an antiseptic in operating rooms and laboratories. Because of this disinfectant property, the violet light is a helpful guardian against infection.

The same imaginative and visual technique may be used to invoke, direct, and become familiar with all the other specialized frequencies associated with the spectrum of color. It takes a great deal of practice to be able to use these specialized frequencies effectively, and it is recommended that students practice with them as often as possible. However, it is not advisable to practice with more than two frequencies or colors at any one practice period because the more frequencies used at one time the more confusing identification and recognition of the energies becomes. Development of the ability to distinguish between the various frequencies involves more than the sense of sight; it is possible and desirable to make use of the other senses and not to seek only to see the colors. One of the objectives of this work in the scientific use of energy is to learn to distinguish and be able to identify frequencies by using any or all of the extended perceptions.

The following brief statements about the various energies, recognized or described in terms of color, offer a few clues to their action and usefulness; it is enough for a beginning:

Violet: A healing energy with capacity to neutralize infection and promote recovery from illness. It should always be followed by the use of white to remove any excess of violet in the vehicles. On some levels it becomes the "Christ Light."

Silver: A nourishing, sustaining energy. It promotes growth, heightens responsiveness, and increases sensitivity to impression and subjective awareness. It decreases emotionalism.

Gold: A pervasive, persuasive, protective energy. It lifts up all that can or will be raised and eliminates that which hinders. On the outer field it becomes a powerful protection from horizontal impacts.

Pink: The energy of love and goodwill. It is useful for the healing of misunderstandings and cleavages, for the creation of harmony and an attitude of goodwill.

Purple: A powerful energy which strengthens the purpose, ambition and determination. It relates to will and power.

Blue: An energy which stimulates, calms and clears thought processes and assists the faculties of the concrete mind and strengthens aspiration and devotion.

Green: An energy required for creative expression and for the manifestation or formulation of anything on lower levels. Also, an energy essential for renewal; it has healing and quieting properties and is necessary for cooperation.

Red: An energy which increases endurance, physical strength, and the
ability to take action. It will strength-
en muscles, improve circulation and
the heart.

Orange: An energy associated with the
vitality; it feeds the whole nervous
system and the concrete mind. A very
stimulating energy.

It should be remembered that each color exists
in a great many shades and tints—a whole spectrum in the one color—from the merest suggestion of the color to the most intense and deepest
shade of the color. In choosing a color with which
to work, select the middle shade of the color. This
selection will provide more contrast when
working with two colors and assist in distinguish-
ing between them.

Protective Techniques

Protection begins with the *Soul Mantram,*
which produces objective identification with the
Soul. Its use begins to apply the Law of Soul Life
in the individual who uses it and makes it a part of
himself.

A similar form of protection is the use of the
Mantram of Unification. Originally, the
Mantram of Unification was the mantram of protection used by that far-distant group who left
personal life and attachment in Atlantis for a dangerous and uncertain journey into an unknown
future. This is also suggested for use as a daily

protective technique. Like those Atlantean disciples and aspirants, we must journey into the future because, like them, we know something of what is coming and therefore something of our destiny.

To offset the currents of fear in mass conscious humanity, to which the disciple is continually exposed, the energies of JOY may be invoked from the Soul. This energy appears as a pale golden color, similar to the color of ginger ale, and contains sparkling bubbles of energy. This energy is invoked by identifying with the Soul and stating: "The nature of the Soul is joy. As the Soul, I invoke the energies of joy." Visualize the energy coming from the Soul Star, filling the Central Channel and, when the channel is filled, irradiating the vehicles and Causal field.

To build a protective globe of energy on the outside of the field to shield the disciple from accidents and intruding harmful forces, the GOLDEN LIGHT should be invoked from the Soul Star. When this technique is followed on a daily basis it will protect the disciple against environmental impacts.

To offset emotional impacts, the disciple should invoke the SILVER energy, drawing it down from the Soul Star to fill the Central Channel. Visualize the silver energy radiating outward to form a protective shield or belt of energy around the solar plexus area.

Of course, all students, by the time they have reached this point, should be very familiar with the use and benefits of the *Whirlwind or spiritual vortex.* This is the disciple's most easily invoked Soul tool and should be used throughout the day and whenever around people.

Along with the above techniques an attitude should be adopted by the disciple toward his personal affairs. That attitude can best be summed up by what Dwal Khul has said in <u>Discipleship in the New Age</u>, Volume II, page 44 and <u>Telepathy</u>, pages 196-197:

> The disciple has to take himself as he is, at any time, with any given equipment, and under any given circumstances; he then proceeds to subordinate himself, his affairs and his time to the need of the hour—particularly during the phase of group, national or world crisis. When he does this within his own consciousness and is, therefore, thinking along lines of the true values, he will discover that his own private affairs are taken care of, his capacities are increased and his limitations are forgotten . . .

> There is a certain esoteric Mantram which embodies this attitude—the attitude of the disciple who is striving, in cooperative endeavor with others, to link hierarchical intent with human aspiration and thus bring humanity nearer to its goal. The intent of the Hierarchy is to increase men's *capacity for freedom* in order to function effectively with that "life more abundantly" which the Christ will bring and which demands that the spirit of man be free— free to approach divinity and free also to choose the Way of that approach. The Mantram bears the name, "The Affirmation of the Disciple." It involves certain inner recognitions and acceptances which are readily perceived by those

whose intuition is sufficiently awake; but its meaning should not be beyond the ability of any sincere student and thinker to penetrate if it appeals to them as significant and warranting their effort.

AFFIRMATION OF THE DISCIPLE

I am a point of light within a greater Light.
I am a strand of loving energy within the stream of Love divine.
I am a spark of sacrificial Fire, focussed within the fiery Will of God.
And thus I stand.

I am a way by which men may achieve.
I am a source of strength, enabling them to stand.
I am a beam of Light, shining upon their way.
And thus I stand.

And standing thus, revolve
And tread this way the ways of men,
And know the ways of God.
And thus I stand.

CHAPTER VII

THE BASIC GROUP MEDITATION

Once the Central Channel is built, the Soul proceeds to use it for many functions with which the aspirant need not be concerned at first. It is our hope that those who are able will pass on what they have learned and assist those who come to them. This involves the beginnings of group activity and consciousness, and hopefully, when at least nine are working together, *group integration*. Group integration refers to a conscious union of the higher principles and may not be recognized by many whose higher principles are so involved. This was a principle goal for those to whom Dwal Khul addressed the letters and text of the two volumes of Discipleship in the New Age. It was *not* successful then as he stated, but since that time changes in humanity and the influx of new energies has made it possible and enabled us to accomplish such an integration in our group, now called by the Brothers the

Prototype Group.

Since what we propose is grouping, beginning with one or two and leading finally to conscious group cooperation, we add here what we have used for years, outlined as a basic group meditation.

We have been told that many energies can only be contacted and used in group formation. There are several things which can be inferred from this statement:

1. That there might be dangers in an attempt to use them individually;

2. That they might relate only to group activity, attitude and purpose;

3. That they are of high order and require united strength, action and devotion to invoke;

4. That no single individual can provide the balance of Ray energies required.

Before considering these suggestions in more detail, let us consider why it is possible to work collectively at all. Like man himself, the planet has an etheric body, and, as with man, this body projects slightly beyond the physical. If properly aligned and in proportion to size, the planetary etheric body would extend many miles, possibly forty miles, above the solid Earth surface. In this we live and move and have our being. In this there is continuity of substance (matter-energy of a more subtle nature but still substantial). In this lies the possibility of telepathic interplay and communication and etheric linking generally. In this way we are never far apart or separate.

The human etheric body is built or woven of energy strands or threads, and correspondingly so is the planetary etheric body. Such analogies exist in every department of life and call attention to the Law of Correspondence which must always be used in connection with occult understanding. As with the human etheric body, the strands of energy composing the planetary etheric body are concentrated in certain areas which are the etheric centers of the planet. Between these are stronger bands of energy and the sum total of these constitute the *planetary etheric network* to which we refer and into which we channel energies. We are thus, consciously or unconsciously, a part of the planetary etheric body, and our individual well-being and clearing is a contribution to planetary purification.

There is also a vertical linkage symbolized and implemented by the Central Vertical Channel, and the sum total of these individual linkages constitute the planetary vertical linkage called the Rainbow Bridge or the Planetary Antahkarana. Each incarnated Soul has a thread of this bridge, of this spiritual energy-substance, tiny and invisible except to the highest inner vision. When it is expanded by meditation and the techniques of clearing, it becomes a permanent channel filled with a continual downpour of a shimmering rainbow-like energy, and it is of immeasurable service to humanity and to Hierarchy. This is the vertical arm of the Fixed Cross;

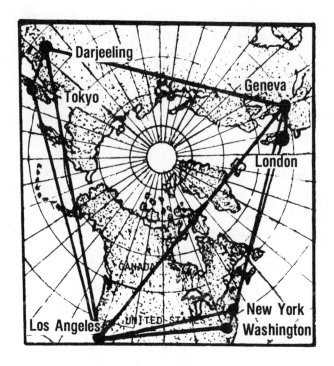

PLANETARY SECOND RAY
TRIANGLE OF POWER

The Planetary Etheric Network is developed in triangles based on this triangle of power which is linked with humanity through the New Group of World Servers and to the Logos through Hierarchy. All meditating groups should link with the nearest point of this triangle to contribute and receive hierarchical energies.

THIS IS THE PLANETARY ANTAHKARANA
THE RAINBOW BRIDGE.

DIAGRAM 17

the horizontal arm provides for the distribution of energy into the planetary network.

Any group meditation is an augmentation, increase, or stimulation of this dual reception and transmission of energy by the intention, attitude and action of the disciples involved. The technique is simple, but its effectiveness requires certain development within disciples – the establishment of a Central Channel of measurable size, and a constantly increasing freedom from accumulated thoughtforms in the vehicles and field.

The diagram of the symbols of group relationships shows the result of increasing numbers and potency. It should be observed that as the number of participants grows, a network or field of energy or light is built.* Also note that there is a space at the center of the odd-numbered groups and a point in the center of the even-numbered groups, and that as the numbers increase, the space gets smaller and approaches a point.

There is a law of nature that whenever a form is built, the ever-present undifferentiated Life

---

* "It will be apparent, therefore, that certain developments must have taken place in the individual before he can consciously become a functioning member of the New Group of World Servers, which is the principal group at this time definitely working under the Law of Group Progress . . . He must have the heart centre awakened, and be so outgoing in his 'behaviour' that the heart is rapidly linked up with the heart centres of at least eight other people. Groups of nine awakened aspirants can then be occultly absorbed in the heart centre of the Planetary Logos." A Treatise on the Seven Rays, Volume II, page 197, by Alice A. Bailey

SYMBOLS OF RELATIONSHIP

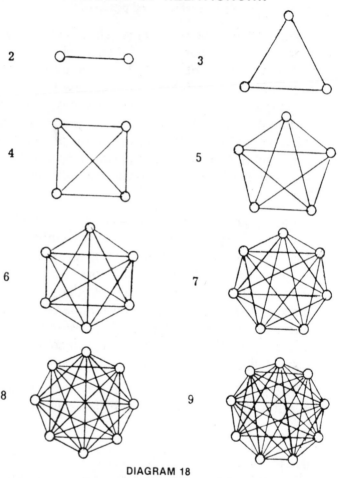

DIAGRAM 18

flows in and expresses itself according to the nature and capacity of the form. Thus, we find at the center a synthetic life-form which we call the Group Soul. The above statement, while fundamental, is over-simplified; that which flows in is of higher and more intense quality, being closer to the One Life, but not identical to it. This is the

NETWORK OF LIGHT

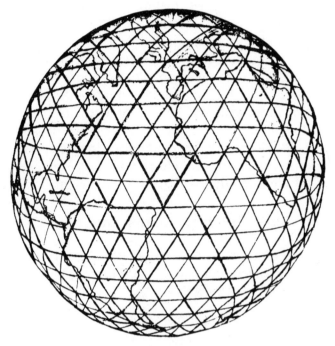

DIAGRAM 19

Planetary Hierarchical Life itself. This infusion is the goal of our group meditation and through it the Soul will become a permanent living entity; by the same rule and process we have defined as a part of the greater form, the planetary etheric body or its specialization, the Planetary Network, is developed and strengthened.

Now the planetary vehicles, like those of its individual human atoms, are clouded and covered with the "fogs and miasmas" precipitating on the physical plane today. There is a desperate need for "bringing in the Light." This process, when carried on with increasing intensity and frequency, will make possible the Externalization of the Hierarchy, the Return of the Christ, and the inauguration of the Aquarian Age. We are told that the Hierarchy is experimenting with many groups; these groups may be identified by their common reference to and identification with the Soul – or with its inner manifestation – the Soul of the planet or the Planetary Hierarchy. Techniques and approaches, recognitions and terminology will vary, but the central identification will always be present.

Basic Group Meditation Outline

All meditations should begin with strengthening the linkage and fusion with the Soul, by saying the Soul Mantram:

"I am the Soul.
I am the Light Divine.
I am Love.
I am Will
I am Fixed Design."

Then strengthen the lines of light from Star to Star which link all members of the group, and the lines of light which link with the Group Soul at the Center. Extend this linkage to those not physically present. Strengthen the bands of light linking the group to other groups which are meeting and meditating for the same purpose; link also with the astral groups and the groups on the plane of the lower mind; link also with the Ashram.

Then say together the Mantram of Unification:

"The sons of men are one, and I am one with
them.
I seek to love, not hate.
I seek to serve and not exact due service.
I seek to heal, not hurt.
Let pain bring due reward of Light and Love.
Let the Soul control the outer form and life and
all events,
And bring to Light the love that underlies the
happenings of the time.
Let vision come and insight.
Let the future stand revealed.
Let inner union demonstrate and outer cleavages
be gone.
Let love prevail.
Let all men love.

Then, as the Soul-infused personal self, the personal self infused by the Soul, as the unified Group, we invoke the One.

Let the energies of Divine Will descend into Hierarchy through the Nirmanakayas, the Divine Contemplatives, the Guardian Wall. These energies become, in Hierarchy, the seven energies of Spiritual Will centered in the Great Chohans who command and evoke from Humanity and Earth the energies of substance and matter, which rise from deepest Earth with the cooperation of the devas, through the New Group of World Servers and groups such as this and their Communicators   into   Hierarchy   where   the

highest and lowest meet and merge and blend
through the Power, the Sound, the Love and the
Will of the Lord of the Seventh Ray.

Let the blended energies descend into the great
magnetic centers of Earth:

Los Angeles, New York, Washington,
London, Geneva, Tokyo, and Darjeeling.

The Will to synthesis, the Will to sacrifice, the
Will to love, the Will to good, the Will to cooperate and harmonize, the Will to know and to act,
the Will to create and to stand, the Will to organ-
ize and to externalize, and the energies of the
governing sign, through the Sun to the ruling
planets, to the Earth, to the magnetic centers of
the Earth, to the disciples and to the magnetic
centers of the disciples.

We welcome the attending devas; let them do
their part; build the thoughtforms, extend the
network, ground the energies, balance the forces,
and with us, command and evoke from deepest
Earth the energies of substance and matter,
which rise into the Great Centers of Earth where
the highest and lowest of the Cosmic Physical
Plane meet, merge and blend into an effective
synthesis with the Power, the Sound, the Love,
and the Will of the Lord of the Seventh Ray.

Let the blended energies go forth into the
Network from center to center, linking the
centers in rivers of radiant life and living light,
from:

Los Angeles to New York, to Wash-

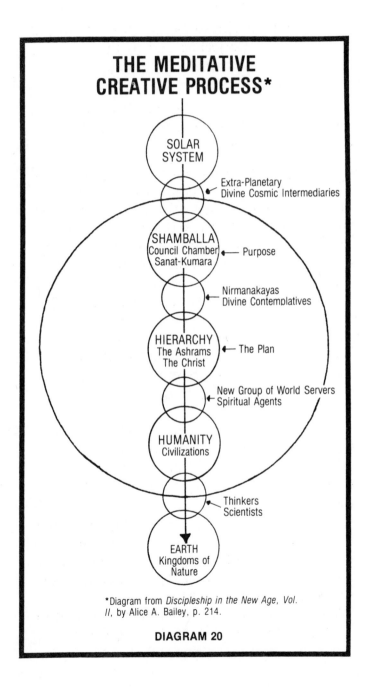

THE MEDITATIVE CREATIVE PROCESS*

SOLAR SYSTEM

Extra-Planetary
Divine Cosmic Intermediaries

SHAMBALLA
Council Chamber
Sanat-Kumara

Purpose

Nirmanakayas
Divine Contemplatives

HIERARCHY
The Ashrams
The Christ

The Plan

New Group of World Servers
Spiritual Agents

HUMANITY
Civilizations

Thinkers
Scientists

EARTH
Kingdoms of
Nature

*Diagram from *Discipleship in the New Age, Vol. II*, by Alice A. Bailey, p. 214.

DIAGRAM 20

ington; London to Geneva, Geneva to
Tokyo to Darjeeling and to the great
Second Ray triangle: Darjeeling to Los
Angeles to Geneva to Los Angeles.

Let these great triangles be filled with Light
and Love and Power and bring an end to that
which is no longer needed.

In the wisdom of Hierarchy, under the control
of the Brothers, the Guardians of the Network,
and in the name of the Christ, let the energies go
forth from the Network to the crisis points on the
planet and to the groups and workers for Humanity and Hierarchy at the crisis points. Let the
vision of these disciples be opened so that they
may recognize and use the available energies. Let
their minds be illumined and inspired so that they
may make right decisions. Let them have the
courage of their convictions and act accordingly.
Let their rightfully conceived plans succeed. Let
them find and know each other and cooperate.
Let the energies form protective shields about
their vehicles. Let communication be established
between them and between the inner and outer
groups through their Communicators. Let the
necessities of life on the physical plane be available to the disciples according to their needs
through these times of crisis. Let any opposition
to their work, or interference in their lives, or
interference with the outgoing energies of Hierarchy in the process of Externalization, be dis-
solved and the forms thereof destroyed by the
White Light of the One. LET THIS DOOR WHERE
EVIL DWELLS BE CLOSED AND SEALED.

At this point, if the meditating group is meeting either three days before, the day of, or three days after the Full Moon,† the group approaches the Ashram of the Master. As the unified group you pass down the Golden Pathway through the ivory door with its center of blue, which expands and through which the group passes *together* in their higher principles to stand in the presence of the Master. Together, the group pledges itself, without reservation, to the service of Humanity and Hierarchy. The Master turns towards Humanity and leads in The Great Invocation:

"From the point of Light within the Mind of God
Let light stream forth into the minds of men.
Let Light descend on Earth.

From the point of Love within the Heart of God
Let love stream forth into the hearts of men.
May Christ return to Earth.

From the center where the Will of God is known
Let purpose guide the little wills of men—
The purpose which the Masters know and serve.

From the center which we call the race of men
Let the Plan of Love and Light work out
And may it seal the door where evil dwells.

Let Light and Love and Power restore the Plan on Earth."

---

†This approach to the Ashram is only made during the Full Moon meditations. Dwal Khul has given instructions on meditation in detail in Discipleship in the New Age, Volume II, pages 113-239.

There follows a silent meditation period of approximately five minutes during which time the thoughtform of the descending energies is held by the group.

We have found that many individuals are not trained in meditation or concentration. Consequently, we do not use long periods of silent meditation, since by observation we have found that attention begins to wander and individuals drop out after five to ten minutes. Therefore, it may be helpful for group leaders to talk out the meditation in order to keep the attention of the group members focused and unified.

Our Prototype Group meditation here given, developed over a period of fifteen years, consists of the following basic principles:

1. Raising the consciousness to the highest point possible;

2. Directing the invoked energies to the Great Triangles or centers of the planet;

3. Distributing the energies to the working disciples of the planet;

4. Blocking of negative forces;

5. Protection of the working disciples;

6. Implementation of the outgoing energies with The Great Invocation;

7. Special projects. (As soon as the meditating group reaches a degree of integration, they will be given Hierarchical projects.)

Meditations will change as groups become more integrated. Like individuals, the higher energies cannot be handled at first. However, all meditations should develop along similar lines.

1. Raising consciousness as high as possible. Development will regulate the effectiveness of this, but should not deter or interfere with the effort;

2. Bringing the energies down to whatever level they are to be used on;

3. Distributing the energies as invoked and evoked.

After a group has formed, having completed the Phase I technique, it may be possible to supply the group leader or leaders with more specific information regarding the group meditation. Group leaders should write to the address given at the end of this book if so interested.

There have been requests for additional information about meditation. We refer to Dwal Khul's large book on that subject. Our own application of such teachings resulted in the meditation given. It should be recognized that there is much in our meditation as given which does not follow the conventional pattern, but represents a way of thinking which involves Earth, Personality, Soul, Spirit and Logos as word phrases. Energies and forces are gathered together from above and below and dispersed by word forms (meditation) to serve Hierarchy and humanity. Group leaders seeking additional information on this subject should contact the post office box given at the end of the book.

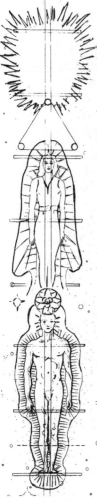

THE GREAT INVOCATION

FROM THE POINT OF LIGHT WITHIN THE MIND OF GOD
LET LIGHT STREAM FORTH INTO THE MINDS OF MEN.
LET LIGHT DESCEND ON EARTH.

FROM THE POINT OF LOVE WITHIN THE HEART OF GOD
LET LOVE STREAM FORTH INTO THE HEARTS OF MEN.
MAY CHRIST RETURN TO EARTH.

FROM THE CENTER WHERE THE WILL OF GOD IS KNOWN
LET PURPOSE GUIDE THE LITTLE WILLS OF MEN.
THE PURPOSE WHICH THE MASTER KNOWS AND SERVES.

FROM THE CENTER WHICH WE CALL THE RACE OF MEN
LET THE PLAN OF LOVE AND LIGHT WORK OUT.
AND MAY IT SEAL THE DOOR WHERE EVIL DWELLS.

LET LIGHT AND LOVE AND POWER
RESTORE THE PLAN ON EARTH.

ANTAHKARANA

DIAGRAM 21

CHAPTER VIII

NEW RELEASES

THE HEAVENLY BRIDE

Quite recently a great individualized deva told us, without explaining, "Watch for the descent of the Heavenly Bride."

There are many mystical thoughtforms about angels and the angelic hosts, but very little about their real nature and place in evolution. This is perhaps largely due to the drastic rules laid down by the Logos and implemented by Hierarchy at the destruction of Atlantis.

Little is actually known of Atlantis and the humanity of that period, long dominated by the influence of the Fourth Root Race. In order to get a glimpse of the nature of this race, we must step into the realm of fantasy. It is a good exercise to do this because the dawning Sixth Subrace of the

Fifth Root Race will be like Atlantis on a higher
turn of the evolutionary spiral.

During the Atlantean culture the range of self-
conscious entities varied widely, from those
barely above the animal kingdom to those of
Second Degree Initiate status. The race as a
whole was emotionally polarized and used the
mind only as an aid to the satisfaction of desire.
Creative thought was demonstrated only by
Initiates and the affairs of the planet were run by
First and Second Degree Initiates (the Hierarchy
of the time) and led by those of the Third Degree.

The entire race of Atlanteans was clairvoyant,
on both astral and etheric levels. The invisible
kingdoms of nature and the subjective energies
and beings not visible to us were part of their
lives and were so accepted. Thus, the angelic
(deva) kingdom was an objective part of their
lives.

The cultures of Atlantis varied widely and, at
their best, were far more luxurious and technically advanced than our own, for the leaders,
through their understanding of the embodied
natural forces, the devas, were able to develop
and control inexhaustible energy sources. Anti-
gravitational energy and scientific devices which
would more than rival our own were common—
the gifts of the Masters.[†]

In the latter days of the race, the lesser initiates

[†] It is known that under Hierarchical control there are under-
ground museums with specimens of such devices preserved for the
benefit of the Aquarian Age at some future date.

became divided into those who accepted the teachings of their spiritual leaders and those who refused to take the next evolutionary step. This division grew into open warfare, involving the use of the natural forces to a point where loss of control destroyed the cultures, races and even the continents themselves.

The forces of Hierarchy then withdrew from open contact and beneficent control of humanity; clairvoyance was cut off to force humanity to use the mind, and the deva kingdom was separated from communication and direct cooperation with human beings. To the next root race, our own, the devas became merely a mythical ideal. This attitude toward the devas will change rapidly during the coming decade.

Many dramatic attempts have been made by imaginative writers to describe Atlantis, but few have suspected the reality. The tales of the Arabian Nights are not far from reality. If thoughtful consideration is given to the above paragraphs, it can be seen that conditions portrayed by the Arabian Nights may have been possible.‡

The story of Aladdin and his wonderful lamp is a symbolic story of Atlantis:

---

‡Dwal Khul has said that whatever man can imagine is true somewhere in the universe.

Allah: Will and intention

Djinn: Devic or natural forces

Lamp: Matter

Oil: Concentrated energy

Flame: Activating fire of mind,
                  imagination

Rubbing: Fire by friction, the nature
                  of matter

The first differentiation from absolute space was the duality *Spirit-Matter.* On our planet, humanity represents the positive aspect or spirit, and the deva kingdom represents the negative aspect, or matter. Since all classifications are relative, humanity is composed of both human and devic elements, and the devas are composed of both devic and human elements to some extent. In fact, in the initiate degrees, both kingdoms take incarnations in the other kingdom in order to learn to work together. (Ordinarily, the deva kingdom is *feminine* to the human's *masculine* energy.)

Thus, the "Descent of the Heavenly Bride" is the return of the Devic Hierarchy or the descent of the devas into open contact and cooperation with humanity again. This reinstatement of contact began in 1975 at the June Convocation[*]

---

[*] Each year after the Christ Full Moon Festival the Hierarchy (and disciples in their higher principles) meet in "Convocation" for the purpose of outlining plans for the coming yearly cycle and encouraging disciples. At the June, 1975 Convocation, for the first time since the destruction of Atlantis, the Devic Hierarchy joined the Human Hierarchy in Convocation.

when nine Devic Masters joined nine human Masters in the organization of the plan for Externalization. Disciples will recall that the Christ is the "leader and teacher of *angels* and men."

The new relationship between the devas and humanity requires many experiments whose results are carefully assessed by the Masters. The Atlantean mistakes of the past will not be permitted. The misuse of the devas will either be blocked or the results will be such that misuse will never occur again.

The basic polarity of the planet is the relationship between the devic and human kingdoms. Representing the "mother" aspect, devas build *all* forms. We have had much contact with the devas in our lives and even with some of the great individualized devas of the Fifth Initiation and beyond, but they did not reveal themselves as individualized until after they were released to communicate in 1975. In most cases they seemed to be unable to communicate except through color and responses somewhat like unusually intelligent domestic animals, with telepathic response such as we often find in such animals. To be addressed telepathically in *words* was a surprise, particularly by a Deva Master.* Indeed, one deva of a great magnetic center was revealed to be a Nirmanakaya, beyond a Master, staying here only to assist Hierarchy and Humanity during the Changeover period.

---

*In the angelic kingdom there were entities of many grades and types with great individualized devas as leaders.

There is little more we can say now regarding the vast amounts of information we are receiving through many members of our group beyond the hints given here. We do not yet know what will be released publicly on this subject. Possibly after world conditions are more peaceful and the promoters of warfare are out of the picture more information can be safely given out.

Ultimately, the goal is for humanity, Hierarchy and the devas to function as one, in a cooperative endeavor to implement the Plan of the Logos, and to build the New Age.†

---

†Those who wish to know more about the devas are referred to Geoffrey Hodson's books, as well as what the Tibetan has written in A Treatise on Cosmic Fire under "Thought Elementals and Fire Elementals."

CONCLUSION

We repeat: The Brothers have said that it is most important to Hierarchy to have as many individuals as possible build the Central Vertical Channel, as described in the first book published in 1975 and distributed steadily ever since.

The added second phase techniques given in this book describe the techniques which will clear the field to the point illustrated in Color Plate 8 and the back cover. This accomplishment will save lives of incarnated effort.

The second phase techniques can be continued after external hindrances are removed and by such use the dark internal patterns and structures will gradually disappear, even without accelerating techniques. When a student reaches the place where further instructions are necessary, they will be available, even if publication may not be desirable or possible for some years.

The student should continue to use the Soul Mantram. This statement is a part of Dwal Khul's first meditation as given in Discipleship in the New Age, Volume II, and it is the heart of *all* successful techniques. Build the Central Channel and use the spiritual vortex as instructed in this book.

It may be difficult to keep up the meditative techniques in the trying days ahead, but little effort is necessary to improve one's self and circumstances, and groups will have much assistance from both the Devic and Human Hierarchies.

As we close this book, we are reminded by a Deva Master that the Four Horsemen have already descended. We were told that the collapse of the world financial system would probably occur this year. Disciples of a certain grade have known that the crisis called Armageddon would occur in this century. There was a time in the 1930's when disaster seemed imminent, however the work of Hierarchy deferred the time of crisis. It does not appear that it can be deferred any longer.

The dawn is near. Do not fear when world conditions produce despair and hopelessness. The world housecleaning which occurs at the end of each race and subrace is benign. The mantram on page 239 of A Treatise on White Magic will be helpful to offset conditions of fear:

"Let Reality govern my every thought
and Truth be the Master of my life."

Learn to accept and transmit Spiritual Will. This is embodied in the words of the Christ, "Thy Will be done." Know, feel and use this mantram of power. THE OPPORTUNITY IS GREAT. The Christ and His Masters are NOW on the physical plane (1982) and the mantram could be "In the Name of the Christ and by the Power of His Name and Sword, let the reality of His presence govern my every thought and His Truth be the Master of my life." This adds to the Invocation of Humanity and when this is strong enough THE CHRIST WILL APPEAR.

Regarding Future Teachings

We are at a time in these "latter" days when events in the immediate future (1981) may make it impossible for us to print and distribute another book. If the techniques of the first two phases are properly used, there will come a time when additional teaching is needed because of the cleared fields and changes in the etheric vehicles of the disciple. At this time assistance from Hierarchy can be counted upon.

We have said that the usual condition of the fields and vehicles interferes seriously with meditative and yoga practices. The Brother's statement that several lives of incarnated effort were saved by the completed Phase I and II techniques confirms our opinion.

Accordingly, when the disciple has completed Phase I and II, there should be little difficulty in using the techniques given by Dwal Khul. It is possible that Fourth and Sixth Ray disciples might be more responsive to the Master Hilarion's suggestions in When the Sun Moves Northward or those in a book published in 1930 called Unsigned Letters of an Elder Brother. This book relates to what would be part of the last phases of our Rainbow Bridge series.

In connection with the book Unsigned Letters of an Elder Brother, the cyclic crisis coming at the end of the 2,500 and the 25,000 year cycle, based on all current data, may be offset by the efforts of Hierarchy itself which was the case in the 30's, or by an unexpected response by humanity as in 1942. The postponement of the crisis called Armageddon has been of inestimable value as generations of the New Group of World Servers become mature and other gains which make the Externalization possible before 1985 as we have been told. This last book could serve for all the instruction needed if the disciple makes the changes necesary to clear his own understanding.

Dwal Khul said at the 1977 convocation, "Personalities have learned how to build the Antahkarana . . ." The processes given in THE RAINBOW BRIDGE have brought thousands to the point of purification and clearing where the techniques given by Dwal Khul can be more easily and successfully used. It is a bridging process done under His injunction to "modify, qualify and adapt" the teachings.

THE RAINCLOUD OF
KNOWABLE THINGS

"There is to be found today in the realm of intuition much of wonder; this can be contacted. It is now the privilege of the race to contact that 'raincloud of knowable things' to which the ancient seer Patanjali refers in his fourth book; the race through its many aspirants, can today precipitate this 'raincloud' so that the brains of men everywhere can register the contact. Hitherto this has been the privilege of the illumined and rare seer. In this way the New Age will be ushered in and the new knowledge will enter into the minds of humanity.

"This can be practically demonstrated if those who are interested . . . can attune themselves to think clearly, and with a poised and illumined mind seek to understand what is relatively a new aspect of truth."

This wonderful privilege requires nothing but an honest need for the truth. It is a gift to humanity! The "Affirmation of the Disciple" on page 191 of this book assists the disciple in gaining the attitude that allows him to contact the "Raincloud of Knowable Things". On page 196-7 of "Telepathy" by Alice A. Bailey is a clear statement of what must be done: "The disciple has to take himself as he is, at any time, with any given equipment, and under any given circumstances; he then proceeds to subordinate himself, his affairs and his time to the need of the hour — particularly during the phase of group, national or world crisis. When he does this within his own consciousness and is, therefore, thinking along the lines of true values, he will discover that his own private affairs are taken care of, his capacities are increased and his limitations are forgotten.''

When the contact with the intuition is first made the impulse is to go deeper into the beautiful realms; if that is done, all you will remember is that you had a wonderful experience. If you stand on the threshold; "And standing thus revolve, and tread this way the way of men, and know the way of God"; you will get the answer you want always.

The contact is most easily made by synchronously meditating groups, though do not think it is too difficult for individuals. It was reached by the author long before he was cleared of patterns, and before he knew not to ask foolish questions, which were answered just the same.

For more information on the "Raincloud of Knowable Things" see the following references to books by Alice A. Bailey:

Esoteric Psychology, Vol. I, p. 12
Telepathy and the Etheric Vehicle, p. 196-7
The Light of the Soul, pages 38, 424-5

Norman Stevens 11/87

Publication and distribution of THE RAINBOW BRIDGE has been successful, that is, the book has reached many First Degree Initiates who are disciples of sufficient evolutionary development to recognize and undertake the work which relates to the First Rule in WHITE MAGIC, page 51, and COSMIC FIRE, page 997. And more importantly, groups have been formed to use the techniques given. Within the period of one year, since the first publication date, several thousand disciples have begun the work of invoking and blending the down pouring energies of Soul and Spirit with the evoked forces of substance and matter. The Synthesis of these energies pours directly into the Plan of Externalization of the Spiritual Hierarchy. Not all have seen or read the book, but all have contacted the thought form on the level of the concrete mind and are responding to its purpose by "modifying, qualifying and adapting the idea as it seems best to them.

We strongly encourage the formation of groups. We are happy to provide additional instructions in this regard. Individual inquiries are also welcome. However, we cannot guarantee that each will be answered personally.

Rainbow Bridge Productions
P.O. Box 929
Danville, CA 94526 USA

The following books are available from Rainbow
Bridge Productions and many New Age bookstores.
Included in this list are the books referred to in this
book, and others recommended by its authors.

The Rainbow Bridge, Phase I
- Link With the Soul
soft cover, 125 pages $6.95

The Rainbow Bridge, Phase II
- Link With the Soul - Purification
soft cover, 244 pages $10.95
hard cover, 238 pages $14.95

Rainbow Bridge Visualization
soft cover, 44 illustrations/pages $7.95

The work of Henry T. Laurency has recently been
translated into English, and is highly recommended
for advanced students of esoteric knowledge.

The Knowledge of Reality
Henry T. Laurency
soft cover, 307 pages $14.95
A straightforward account of the esoteric world
view, it covers Western philosophy, true history,
anthrosophy, and yogic philosophy.

The Philosopher's Stone
Henry T. Laurency
hard cover, 352 pages $23.95
Based on Pythagoras' Hylozoics, this is a complete
knowledge system that covers cosmic to individual
laws of life, the Will to Unity, and esoteric culture.

Booklets by Henry T. Laurency:

Introduction to Esoteric Philosophy	$2.50
Meditation	$2.50
Gnostics	$2.50
Gnostic Symbols	$2.50
Identification and Liberation	$2.50
Discipleship	$4.50
The Planetary Hierarchy	$4.50

The Secret Doctrine
H. P. Blavatsky
2 volume facsimile edition

soft cover	$18.00
hard cover	$21.00

When the Sun Moves Northward
Mabel Collins

soft cover	$4.75

Light on the Path
& Through the Gates of Gold
Mabel Collins

soft cover	$6.00

Unsigned Letters of an Elder Brother
Elder Brother

soft cover	$8.95

Brotherhood of Angels and Men
Geoffrey Hodson

soft cover	$5.95

These books are the textbooks from which the Rainbow Bridge work is derived. The Rainbow Bridge techniques are practical applications of Dwal Khul's writings, following his injunction to "modify, qualify, and adapt" the teachings.*

Books by Alice A. Bailey:

The Consciousness of the Atom	$7.00
The Destiny of Nations	$7.00
Discipleship in the New Age Vol. I	$20.00
Discipleship in the New Age Vol. 2	$18.00
Education in the New Age	$7.00
Externalization of the Hierarchy	$18.00
From Bethlehem to Calvary	$8.00
From Intellect to Intuition	$7.00
Glamour: A World Problem	$9.00
Initiation, Human and Solar	$7.00
Letters on Occult Meditation	$9.00
The Light of the Soul	$12.00
Problems of Humanity	$7.00
The Reappearance of the Christ	$7.00
The Soul and its Mechanism	$7.00
Telepathy and the Etheric Vehicle	$7.00
A Treatise on Cosmic Fire	$30.00
A Treatise on the Seven Rays:	
Vol. I Esoteric Psychology I	$12.00
Vol. II Esoteric Psychology II	$18.00
Vol. IIIEsoteric Astrology	$18.00
Vol. IVEsoteric Healing	$18.00
Vol. V The Rays and the Initiations	$18.00
A Treatise on White Magic	$18.00
The Unfinished Autobiography	$10.00
The Labours of Hercules	$8.00

---

* Discipleship in the New Age Vol. II, p 389

The Agni Yoga Series

Leaves of Morya's Garden:	
Vol. I The Call	$12.00
Vol. II Illumination	$12.00
New Era - Community	$12.00
Agni Yoga	$12.00
Infinity I	$12.00
Infinity II	$12.00
Hierarchy	$12.00
Heart	$12.00
Fiery World I	$12.00
Fiery World II	$12.00
Fiery World III	$12.00
Aum	$12.00
Brotherhood	$12.00

If unsure where to start, "The Call" is a good first choice.

Ordering Information:

Please send orders to the address below. Include $1.75 postage for the first book (or $.75 if ordering only one booklet) and $.75 for each additional book ($.25 for each additional booklet). Canadian orders add $3.00, overseas add $5.00. California and Washington state residents please add 8.25% sales tax.

A free copy of our full catalog can also be obtained by writing to the address below.

Rainbow Bridge Productions
P.O. Box 929
Danville, CA 94526 USA

HIERARCHY

HOW·TO·TRANSMUTE·THE·MOST·BITTER·INTO
THE·MOST·SWEET·?·NAUGHT·SAVE
HIERARCHY·WILL·TRANSFORM·LIFE·INTO·ITS
HIGHER·CONCIOUSNESS. IT·IS·IMPOSSIBLE
TO·IMAGINE·A·BRIDGE·INTO·THE·INFINITE
BECAUSE·A·BRIDGE·IS·IN·NEED·OF·ABUTMENTS.
BUT·HIERARCHY,AS·THE·ABUTMENTS·OF·THE
BRIDGE,BRINGS·ONE·TO·THE·SHORE·OF·LIGHT.
AND·IMAGINE·THE·ENTIRE·EFFULGENCE
THAT·THE·EYES·BEHOLD! AND·UNDERSTAND
THE·SONG·OF·LIGHT.
LET·US·LABOR·FOR·THE·LIGHT·OF

HIERARCHY

"HIERARCHY" AGNI YOGA PRESS 1933